GENTLEMEN, *START YOUR ENGINES!*

THE BONHAMS GUIDE TO CLASSIC SPORTS & RACE CARS

———

by Jared Zaugg

gestalten

CONTENT

THE BONHAMS GUIDE TO CLASSIC SPORTS & RACE CARS

When it comes to rare and important motorcars, Bonhams has always distinguished itself by its depth and breadth. From pioneering motor buggies all the way to futuristic land rockets, our premium offerings across a broad spectrum represent not just one niche aspect of collectors' automobiles but all genres. This is a foundational strength of ours and with our global expertise has allowed us to achieve numerous world records, including the two most valuable cars ever sold at auction.

More than anything, we are passionate motorists and believe, above all else, that cars are meant to be enjoyed. In this spirit, I hope these sports and racing cars serve to inspire.

JAMES KNIGHT
Bonhams Group, Motoring Director

THE FIRST RACE WAS CONCEIVED WHEN THE SECOND CAR WAS BUILT

BY JARED ZAUGG

There's no question the automobile has changed the world—physically, economically, culturally, and emotionally. Its invention and, especially, availability through mass production is one of the greatest revolutions in human history. And one of the most important catalysts in all this was the desire for speed.

The adage "racing improves the breed" was never truer for motor vehicles. The drive to win, to be the fastest, to be the best, to simply go faster, accounts for innumerable advances in the development and evolution of the automobile, benefitting all of today's classes of transportation. If it were not for the spirit of competition, cars as we know them today would not exist.

There are very few things in any contemporary automobile that have not been either directly developed or improved by racing. From basic engine design (the overhead camshaft), transmissions, gearboxes, and tire technology, to independent suspension, superchargers and turbochargers, fuel injection, and push-button ignition, not to mention a host of safety features like disc brakes, roll cages, seat belts, rear-view mirrors, and so much more—even the basic aerodynamic shape of automobiles and the

use of wind tunnels to create more slippery designs—the benefits from the pursuit of swiftness are ever present. Each time we step into even the most mundane of vehicles, we are profiting in some way from the sport of racing and the craving for speed.

Not only that, but racing represents the best of us—ingenuity, competitiveness, perseverance, hope, bravery, sportsmanship, and, sometimes, humility. In race car drivers we see pioneers, people who are willing to risk their lives in the pursuit of not just winning but also breaking records and pushing frontiers. Even more important are race car designers, the innovators whose labors have such far reaching effects.

Perhaps most important of all is the emotional impact of sports and racing cars. Who can forget the first time they saw their "dream car" in person or drove their first sports car? For me, when I finally came face to face with an Aston Martin DB4 GT Zagato, my knees literally went weak. When I first stood next to a Shelby Daytona and heard—and felt—its thunderous roar, my smile was ear to ear despite what seemed like ruptured drums in those ears. Best of all are memories with my father in his

Daimler DB18 Special Sports enjoying the empty country roads. Not just a means of conveyance, sports and racing cars transcend—or defy—practicality and engage all of our five senses. They are the reason motoring is so fun, whether we realize it or not.

As one of the world's leading auction houses, Bonhams has represented an incredible array of racing and sports cars, the collective value of which—in terms of history, culture, engineering, design, and currency—is staggering. After several years of watching so many significant models cross their auction block, I determined a richly illustrated book featuring a selection of these mechanical sculptures was due. While by no means comprehensive (far from it; there is so much more), I hope this collection provokes thought and stirs emotion. This effort is not so much history book as it is art museum.

I would like to thank Robert Klanten for his vision, my parents for instilling in me a love of classic cars (and my brother for motorcycles), my wife for her inspiration, and most of all Malcolm Barber, Bonhams Co-Chairman, for his foresight and contagious passion. I extend my gratitude to everyone at Bonhams for their support, access and enthusiastic assistance. I've never met a team more enamored with and dedicated to the subject of their profession.

Last but not least, I'd like to acknowledge the talented and generous photographers whose images are pictured herein, especially Pawel Litwinski who's contributed the majority. Sincere thanks to him, Tom Wood, Simon Clay, and Michael Furman.

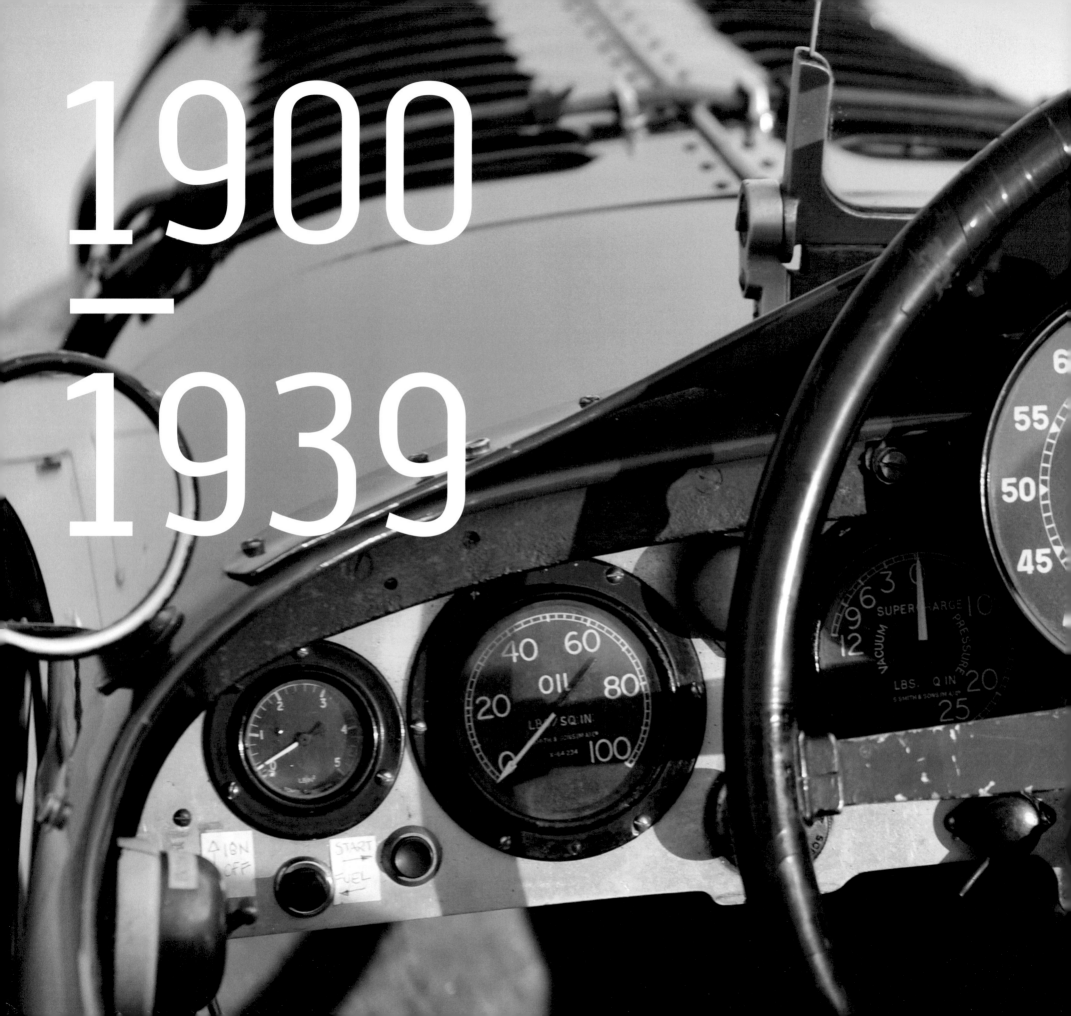

1900
–
1939

1902
DE DIETRICH
16-HORSEPOWER "PARIS-VIENNA"
REAR-ENTRANCE TONNEAU

"It is seldom, if ever, that racing automobiles have done so well on their first appearance."

– *The Autocar*

Forgotten and discovered twice, once in 1940 when a German bomb demolished the English stable in which it was stored and later in 1942 when a notice in a publication led an inquisitive motoring enthusiast on a search, this veteran motorcar has seen its fair share of luck.

With its powerful four-cylinder, 4078 cc motor, this chain-driven, four-seater De Dietrich is identical in specification to those factory racers built for the famous 1902 Paris-Vienna Race. "Same as you can buy" has always been a potent sales tool for automotive makers, who realize that competing in motor sport with examples of their production models is excellent advertising. That was as true in 1902 as it is today, and the excitement ignited by that year's Paris-Vienna Race, which was run concurrently with the Gordon Bennett Trophy (Paris-Innsbruck), saw De Dietrich of Lunéville, in the region of Lorraine,

France, enter four of their new 16 hp cars.

The roots of the De Dietrich company lie in the Alsace region, where in 1681 the mayor Dominique de Dietrich had signed the act that made Strasbourg a French city. Soon after, the de Dietrich family acquired an ironworks at Niederbronn, 26 miles north of Strasbourg, to establish a metallurgy business that by the mid-Nineteenth Century had become a specialized manufacturer of railway wheels, axles and rails. However, after the Franco-Prussian War in 1870, Alsace and part of the neighboring province of Lorraine had been annexed by the victorious Germans, who instituted protectionist customs duties that prejudiced sales to the firm's French customers. To counter this, in 1879 the De Dietrich company set up a French subsidiary in Lunéville, a border town that attracted former citizens of the annexed territories who had chosen exile rather than adopt German nationality.

At the time, the newly opened De Dietrich company of Lunéville had acquired the license to build cars designed

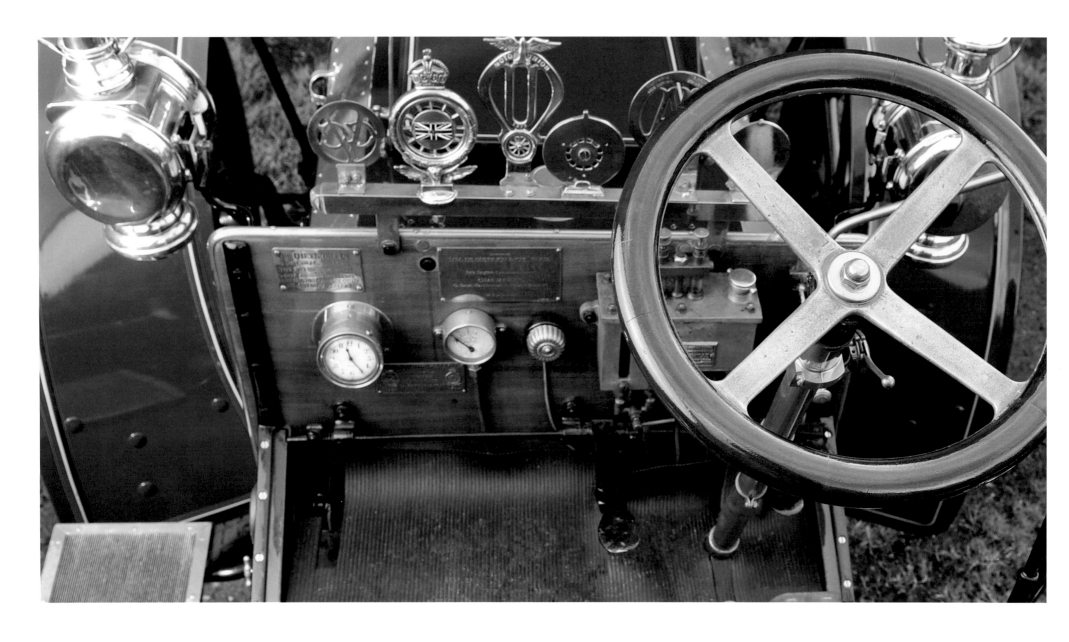

by Amédée Bollée, but these idiosyncratic flat-twin automobiles had become thoroughly outmoded by 1901. Company board member Baron Adrien de Türckheim, whose father had married into the de Dietrich family and ran the Lunéville factory, looked around for an up-to-date successor.

In 1902 de Türckheim visited Nice (likely for the automobile meeting in April of that year) and saw an unfamiliar car that interested him greatly—a Turcat-Méry driven by the crack driver Henri Rougier. Journalist Paul Mayan introduced de Türckheim to the car's makers, cousins Léon Turcat and Simon Méry.

"In the Paris–Vienna Race, De Dietrich performed in a manner so creditable as to astonish automobilists."

They had first built a car as early as 1896 and established a manufacturing company in their hometown of Marseille in 1899. Their latest models had been created for the proposed 418-mile Nice-Abazzia contest in which they were thought likely to "prove one of the revelations of the coming race," but a last-minute adjustment of the weight regulation gave them no chance to prove their mettle. De Türckheim was taken for a drive in one of the new Turcat-Mérys and was so impressed by its design that he took out a license to build them under the De Dietrich name.

In its report on the Nice convention, *The Autocar* disclosed that a Turcat-Méry "had been disposed of to Mr. Guinness, the famous brewer of Dublin" and that the new Turcat-Mérys were "really splendid vehicles." It further added: "We were informed that the car has been timed to run at the rate of 52 to 55 mph on good level roads. It is certainly very fast, and we were given an opportunity to try the vehicle with a run through Nice and down to the seafront, where the motor showed a great elasticity and the speeds were changed promptly with perfect ease."

The Autocar also waxed lyrical about the 16 hp De Dietrich (with Turcat-Méry system) when the first examples arrived in Britain in the autumn of 1902: "These fine vehicles are the output of the great firm of De Dietrich and Company of Lunéville, a firm of rolling stock and

locomotive builders whose name is a household word in engineering circles on the continent. As now turned out, the De Dietrich carriage made its first bow to the public in the 1902 Paris-Vienna Race, when three 16 hp cars faced the starter, and all performed in a manner so creditable as to astonish automobilists in general and the older constructors of automobiles in particular. It is seldom, if ever, that racing automobiles have done so well on first appearance. Although combining many of the best points of the latest Panhard and Mercedes construction, the new car nevertheless exhibits much originality in detail."

As noted, an early customer for this automotive newcomer was the Honorable Rupert Guinness, heir to the Earl of Iveagh, who in the spring of 1903 took delivery of the 16 hp De Dietrich ordered in 1902. The Burlington Carriage Company of London imported the bare chassis from Lunéville and fitted it with their own coachwork, as was the custom of the day.

The handsome Burlington four-seater body fitted to the Guinness car had a detachable tonneau section that could be removed to convert it into a racing two-seater. It was displayed at the March 1903 Cordingley Exhibition in the Agricultural Hall in Islington, where *The Autocar* described it as "one of the finest examples of body building in the show" (but attributed it to the wrong coach-builder, prompting an abject apology in the following issue correctly crediting Burlington for "the exquisite turnout of the whole vehicle," accompanied by a photograph of Mr. Guinness at the wheel).

In 1903, when a canopy and windshield were fitted, the De Dietrich was used as the wedding car for Mr. Guinness and his bride Gwendolen, daughter of the fourth Earl of Onslow. Three years later, Guinness used the De Dietrich, fitted with a closed landaulet body, in his campaign when running as Unionist candidate for the East London Haggerston constituency. But in 1912, the De Dietrich, fitted again with its original tonneau body, was driven into the stable at Guinness' home of Pyrford Court at Woking in Surrey and put up on blocks. There it would stay until 1940 when a bomb dropped during a German World War II air raid demolished the stable. The car was undamaged but was moved to the Guinness dairy farm in Old Woking, where it stood out in the open, "a roosting place for the birds of the air and a plaything for the local brats."

Then, in March 1942, the ever-vigilant Bill Boddy, editor of *Motor Sport*, published a list of 50 veteran, Edwardian, and vintage cars most at risk from the national scrap metal drive. Included in that list was a "De Dietrich, Type 8, four-cylinder Roi de Belge, rough, no tires, big engine, chain drive (Surrey)."

Veteran Car Club (VCC) committee member Francis Hutton-Stott decided it was worth expending what little of the wartime petrol ration remained in the tank of his Morgan 4/4 to investigate and, upon seeing the car, realized from its automatic inlet valves, gilled-tube radiator, and flitch-plated wooden chassis that it could be no later than 1903 in date.

Lord Iveagh (the title to which the Honorable Rupert Guinness had succeeded) was not at home, but Hutton-Stott located the Earl's chauffeur who recommended writing to Lord Iveagh and asking if he would dispose of the car to a good home. The Earl responded that he would be happy to give Hutton-Stott the car without charge if he could arrange transport. A tow truck was quickly called and the car brought to Hutton-Stott's home, where in due course a "firing-up" party was organized with luminaries of the old car world—John Bolster, Bunny Tubbs, Laurence Pomeroy, and Cecil Clutton.

Amazingly, after lying idle for 30 years, the engine fired almost immediately and kept running. Though the clutch was inoperative and the gear lever was missing, Clutton engaged second gear with a screwdriver and was push-started down the drive. Fortunately the clutch freed in time to avert disaster and the car circled a flowerbed in a cloud of smoke "touching a speed that may have been 25 mph but looked three times as fast."

Refurbishment began when the war ended, with the car being completely rebuilt by Teddy Pilmore-Bedford of Catford and Leslie Paget of the Wimbledon Motor Works. Making its debut at the VCC Oxford Rally in May 1950, the car successfully completed its first London-Brighton Run in November that year.

Under Hutton-Stott's stewardship, the De Dietrich took part in several London-Brighton Runs, Edwardian races, and parades at Silverstone and Castle Combe, and made the fastest time of the day at the 1954 VCC Bexhill Speed Trials before going on display in the Montagu Motor Museum at Beaulieu. In 1970, prolific British collector Michael Banfield acquired the car and had it comprehensively and magnificently restored.

Despite being 112 years old, the De Dietrich is a strong and capable runner as demonstrated on many occasions and is, as Editor Boddy of *Motor Sport* wrote in 1961, "a splendid reminder both of the now legendary town-to-town races held at the turn of the century and of the sort of motor car in which the more sporting members of the aristocracy liked to burn the roads in the early days of automobilism."

DE DIETRICH 16-HORSEPOWER
"PARIS-VIENNA" REAR-ENTRANCE TONNEAU

Engine:	4-liter, 4-cylinder	Chassis no.:	1036
Horsepower:	16	Engine no.:	558

Coachwork by Burlington. Paris–Vienna Race specifications.
Formerly owned by Rupert Guinness, Lord of Iveagh.

Sold at Bonhams Goodwood Festival of Speed Sale, Chichester, June 2014 for £998,300—a new world auction record for the marque.

1907
AMERICAN
UNDERSLUNG 50-HORSEPOWER ROADSTER

It represents one of the earliest statements by a manufacturer that their cars were made specifically for sporting use, rather than simple conveyance.

The innovative but short-lived American Motor Car Company of Indianapolis, Indiana, is best remembered today for their famous "underslung" models. These striking designs, developed by Fred Tone and Henry Stutz, inventively placed the frame rails below the axles, providing a significantly reduced center of gravity and excellent handling attributes, not to mention a swift, sporting profile. The problem of ground clearance was remedied by the use of considerably oversized wheels, which were necessary to handle the very poor road conditions of the day.

When it debuted, the profile of the American's underslung chassis was dramatic and memorable—as was the car's position as a luxury automobile and its corresponding price—and it instantly became an icon of both style and performance of the era. These charismatic machines have been prized since the day they were built, evidenced by the list of the cars' owners—a veritable "who's who" of automotive luminaries such as Briggs Cunningham, Larz Anderson, and Bill Harrah.

The Roadster model in particular is one of the most interesting built by the company—and indeed of all cars of this period—because it represents one of the earliest statements by its manufacturer that their cars were made specifically with sporting use in mind, rather than simple conveyance. In 1907, the American Motor Car Company built only one model—the Underslung Roadster. Furthermore, no other US manufacturer offered a gasoline car for speed and sport. The American Underslung Roadster is therefore, arguably, the very first sports car from the United States.

With the slogan "The car for the discriminating few" the elite American Underslung Roadster was revolutionary, fast, luxurious, and expensive, and it remains today one of the most sought-after veteran collector's cars.

Noted American Motor Car collector Frank Deemer of Pennsylvania purchased this Roadster new for his honeymoon. Being in the oil and natural gas business, the then young Deemer choose what he felt to be the best automobile of its kind, and the fact that it was being called by the new term of "sports car" certainly held appeal for him and his new bride.

One night on their trip the young couple parked the car in a barn in Oil City, Pennsylvania. Unfortunately, that night a fire in the barn damaged the new car and rendered it inoperable. But the incident only briefly curtailed the honeymooner's journey, as they simply arranged for the car to be shipped back home while the happy pair hopped a train and headed to American's Indianapolis factory to acquire

23

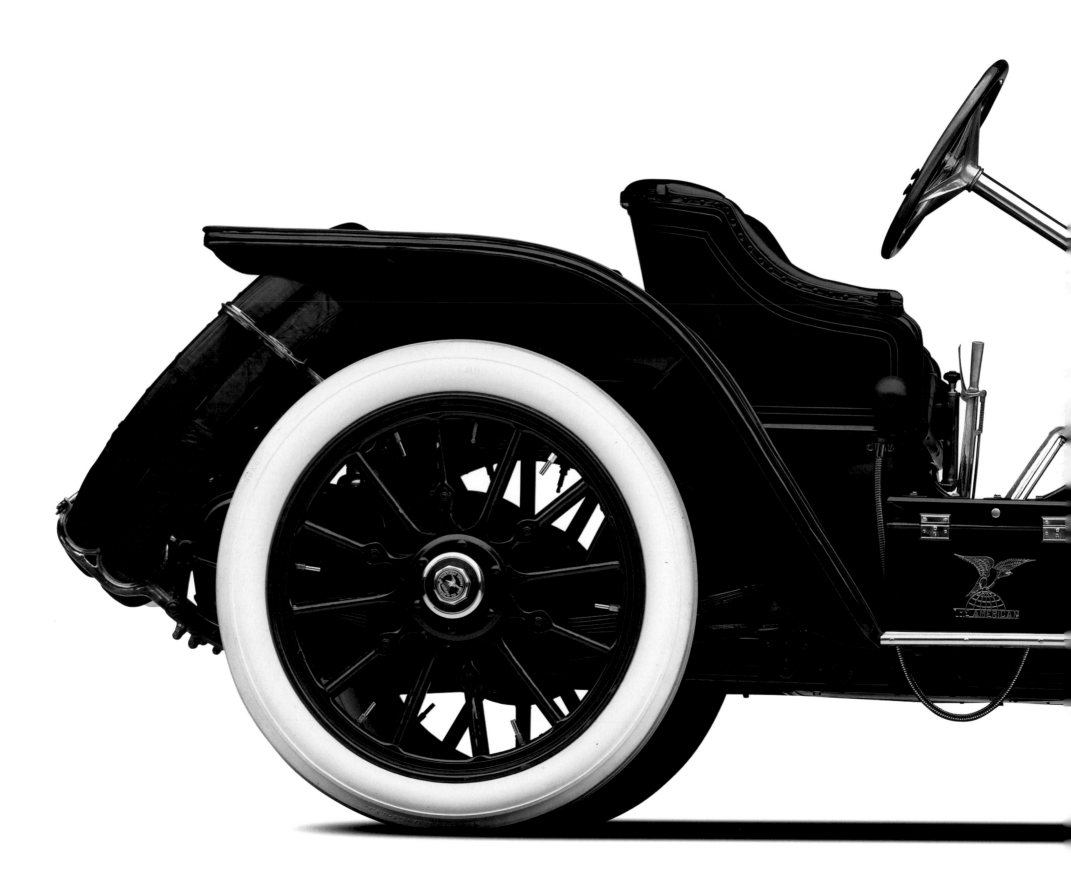

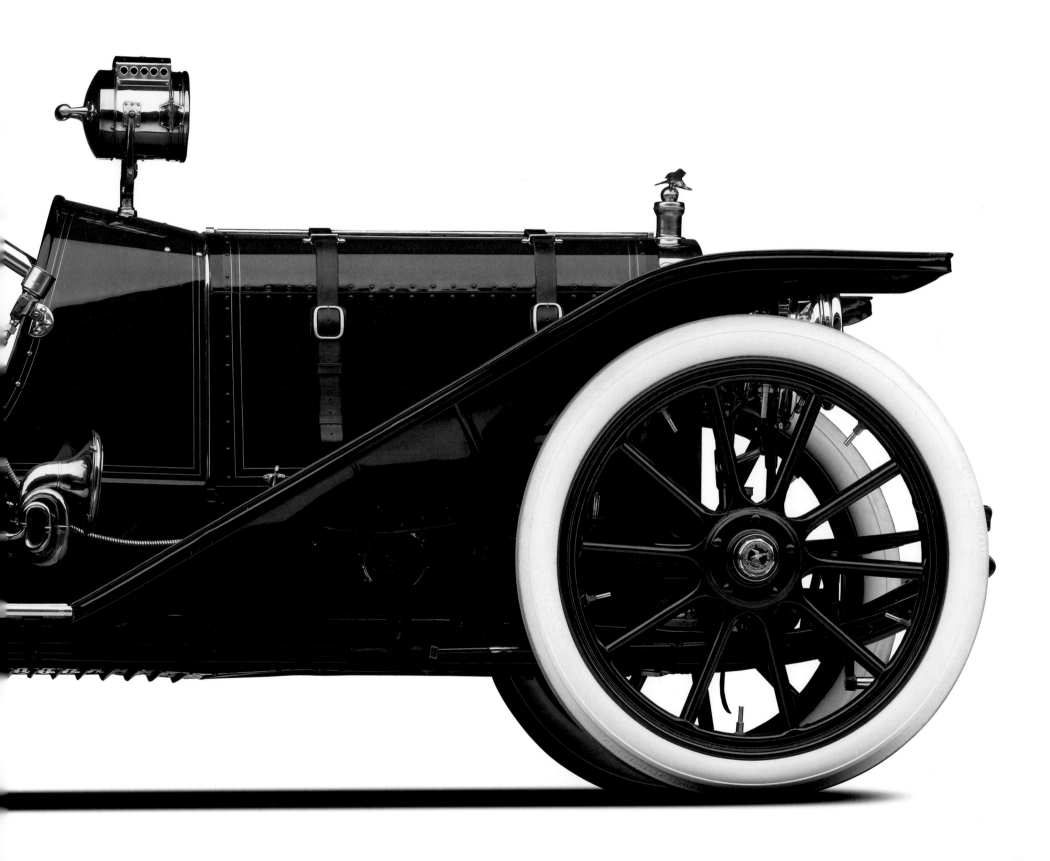

another one in its place. Although over the course of his life Deemer owned at least four Americans, it was said that his honeymoon car was the one that he cherished most.

Over a half-century later, the Roadster was brought out of long-term storage and completely restored by antique automobile enthusiast Walter Seeley, who presented the like-new car to Deemer's son in 1968—a full 60 years after his father and mother blissfully roared along the country roads on their honeymoon.

If one places this car in the context of its contemporaries, it is the equivalent of a jet in an era of turbo-props, with all the defining hallmarks of the great sports cars that have followed, such as the Shelby Cobra. Sitting atop a mere 110-inch (279 cm) wheelbase is a 50 hp, 476.5 ci (7808 cc), four-cylinder, T-head motor, with mechanical valves and four speeds with which to enjoy its sheer

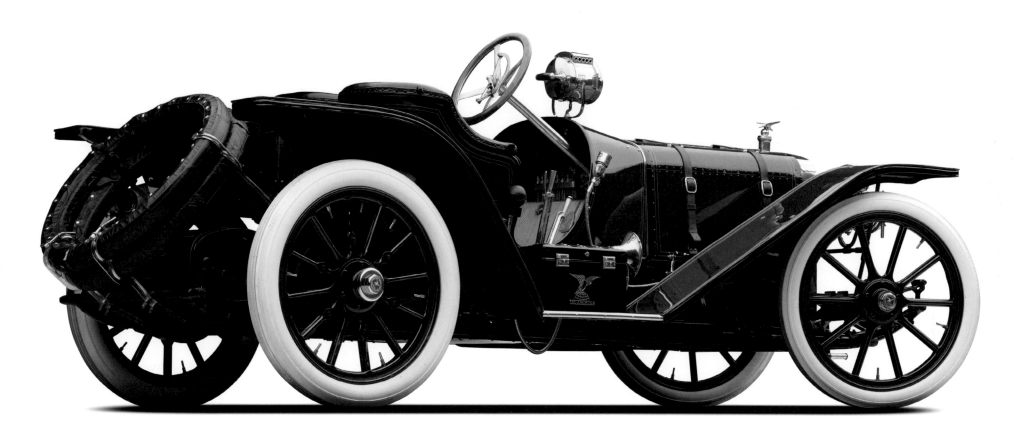

performance. At the dawn of the twentieth century, such motors were usually created to ensure that the chauffeurs of behemoth limousines might convey their passengers at speeds faster than their recently obsolete horses and carriage. With the Roadster, all that power is available for the lucky passengers in its two modest bucket seats.

AMERICAN UNDERSLUNG
50-HORSEPOWER ROADSTER

| **Engine:** | 7.8-liter, 4-cylinder | Engine no.: | 1402 |
| **Horsepower:** | 50 | | |

Coachwork by American. Oldest existing American sports car.

Sold at Bonhams Preserving the Automobile Auction, Philadelphia, October 2014, for $1,430,000—a world auction record for the marque.

1908
ITALA *GRAND PRIX*
FACTORY RACER

"I have no hesitation in saying…
that the Itala is one of the most exciting
cars that has been my lot to drive."

– Kent Karslake

The Itala company was founded in 1904 in Turin, Italy, by Matteo Ceirano and Guido Bigio. Initially, their cars mimicked trendsetting Mercedes designs of the time featuring, for example, advanced shaft drive (rather than the standard chain drive) to a live rear axle. Soon, however, Italia was making a name for itself through competitive prowess when factory driver Alessandro Cagno won the first Targa Florio in Sicily in 1906, and Prince Borghese achieved the now legendary victory in the first Peking-Paris epic in 1907.

Notwithstanding these huge wins for Itala, it was the French Grand Prix—more accurately the Grand Prix de l'Automobile Club de France—that was the most prestigious race of the era, and one in which any manufacturer worth its mettle had to contest.

After the 1907 French GP, an international conference was held in Ostend, Belgium, to discuss a new unified "formula" or set of technical racing regulations to standardize the disparate rules varying between nations and manufacturers. As a result of the welcomed new formula, Itala went to work on building three custom-designed racers (one of which was this very car) under the direction of chief designer Alberto Balloco.

That year the 1908 French GP received entries from no fewer than 17 manufacturers: Baynard-Clement, Brasier, Lorraine-Dietrich, Mors, Motobloc, Panhard-Levassor, Porthos and Renault from France; Benz, Mercedes and Opel from Germany; Germain from Belgium; Austin and Weigel from the United Kingdom; Thomas from the United States; and FIAT and Itala from Italy.

Itala's drivers for its three entries were Cagno, the sometime chauffeur to Queen Margherita of Italy and winner of the Targa Florio, Henri Fournier, winner of the 1901 Paris-Berlin Race, and newcomer Giovanni Piacenza. Although one of the Italas had to retire early due to gearbox trouble, the remaining two ran strong and steady,

coming in after eight grueling hours and 770 kilometers (478.5 miles) later at 11th and 20th place respectively.

After the French GP, the Itala team cars were shipped to Savannah, Georgia, for the American GP road race where they fared little better. On home soil, however, at the Coppa Florio in Bologna, Cagno finished third and salvaged the pride of the marque that had made its name from high performance and reliability.

In 1909, this particular car, thought to have been the one raced by Piacenza, was in the private possession of a Robert Wil-de-Gose who brought it to Brooklands and lapped the circuit at 93.22 mph. The next year he returned and raised the speed to 101.80 mph—faster than the Mercedes that vanquished it in 1908!

Despite its massive size and purpose-bred design, the thunderous four-cylinder, 12-liter Itala was a very man-

ageable and practical automobile. On his first opportunity at driving this car, early Grand Prix historian and author Kent Karslake was totally transfixed, remarking:

"I have no hesitation in saying…that the Itala is not only one of the most exciting cars that has been my lot to drive but also one of the least alarming. How big a car feels to its driver appears to bear no relation to its actual size, and from the point of view of tractability and accurate placing on the road this is a gargantuan that feels like something out of Lilliput.

The steering is of thoroughbred precision with no trace of undue heaviness in spite of the fact that the wheel only needs one complete turn from lock to lock. The gear lever is pushed or pulled, rather than flicked, as if to indicate that there is something pretty solid in the way of pinions on the other end of the mechanism, but it moves with

"Yes, this extraordinarily imposing car plainly embodies everything about which Mr. Toad might have gasped, 'Oh bliss, oh my, oh joy!'"

complete smoothness and the gears change with unfailing ease and silence.

Yet there is one insidious peril in the driving of the car. There is, it must be remembered, 100 hp available to the driver delivered at only 1800 rpm, which means that when the engine is exerting a really tremendous urge, it sounds and feels as if it was doing next to no hard work at all. The effect of this on the driver is an intoxicating sense of power without responsibility. He is tempted to feel that he can do no wrong and, as he sweeps along with this huge surge of power, obedient to the lightest whim of his right toe, to throw back his head and fill the astonished air with echoing peals of Homeric laughter.

Yes, this extraordinarily imposing 1908 Grand Prix Itala plainly embodies everything about which Mr. Toad might have gasped, 'Oh bliss, oh my, oh joy!'"

A later owner, renowned horologist and car collector George Daniels, said of the Itala:

"You have to experience a car like this, no way you can describe it. You've got to do it, and you will either love it or hate it. The tranquility of these early cars is difficult to describe, everything is rotating so slowly…and yet you are really whistling through the atmosphere. It's a wonderful sensation, only doing 1100 rpm and yet it's loping along at 80 mph. Eighty miles per hour! It's the best experience in motoring."

ITALA GRAND PRIX FACTORY RACER

Engine:	12-liter, 4-cylinder	**Chassis no.:**	871
Horsepower:	100	**Engine no.:**	871

Coachwork by W. Vincent. 1 of 3 factory racers built. Raced in the French GP, American GP, Coppa Florio and at Brooklands.

Sold at Bonhams Goodwood Festival of Speed Sale, Chichester, June 2012, for £1,737,500 – a world auction record for the marque.

1913
BUGATTI *TYPE 18*
SPORTS TWO-SEATER

Under capable hands, "Black Bess" was a force to be reckoned with and was able to easily punch above her weight.

Before heading out on his own, prodigy designer Etorre Bugatti had been involved with De Dietrich, Mathis, Hermes, Deutz, Isotta-Fraschini, and FIAT all within the first decade of the twentieth century. So when his second model, the Type 18, debuted it was no surprise that the five-liter, four-cylinder engine reflected design influences from Isotta-Fraschini and FIAT. From 1912 until 1914 only seven examples of the Type 18 were built and this particular car, number 474, was the fourth.

The car was supplied new to renowned French aviator and national hero Roland Garros. In those days all forms of motoring—motorcars, motorcycles, and aeroplanes—were closely intertwined. As exciting, nascent industries they attracted daring, charismatic, wealthy men, usually adept at all three forms of transportation, who risked their lives and fortunes for speed, exhilaration, and glory. The 25-year old celebrity Garros driving an exclusive Bugatti surely must have been a marketing coup for the newly established automotive marque.

Technically, the Type 18 is a fascinating precursor to advancements from Bugatti's design board. The four-cylinder engine displaced 5,027 cc (bore 100 mm and stroke 160 mm) and the single overhead camshaft was driven by a vertical shaft from the front of the three bearing crankshaft. Bugatti's appreciation of the importance of the induction side of the engine resulted in two inlet valves and one exhaust valve per cylinder. Some 100 hp was claimed at 2,400 rpm. Drive is transmitted through a multi-plate, metal-to-metal clutch to a four-speed and reverse gearbox with final drive by exposed side-chains. Discounting contemporary convention, Bugatti adopted double semi-elliptic leaf front springs and reversed quarter elliptic rear springs—shades of things to come. The Type 18 had a potential top speed of 100 mph, but performance could be readily varied by the simple expedient of changing chain sprockets.

For the coachwork, the young pilot commissioned Labourdette to build a sporting two-seater with offset seating that allowed him maximum elbowroom when driving the car with his personal mechanic Jules Hue as passenger.

When completed, it was a mighty exciting motorcar that Garros took delivery of, one which he no doubt drove in spirited fashion.

After Garros was killed in air-to-air combat in the Great War (likely by German ace Hermann Habich) his car changed hands a number of times, including owner Ivy Cummings, the fearless English racing belle who achieved many successes at the wheel of the car she nicknamed "Black Bess" after the horse of legendary highwayman Dick Turpin—a moniker that has forever stuck.

Under capable hands, Black Bess was a force to be reckoned with and was able to easily punch above her weight, going against the larger engines of Itala, FIAT, and Mercedes. Raced hard but honestly during her well-documented series of owners all the way up to 1988, Black Bess

The early motoring industry attracted daring, charismatic, wealthy men who risked their lives and fortunes for speed, exhilaration and glory.

demonstrated time and again the attributes with which she was endowed, proving to be a faithful and tireless warrior.

There are but a handful of significant pre-First World War motorcars with such an impressive and long competition history surviving in complete condition, and this is one of them. Not only that but number 474 is just one of three Type 18s remaining—the other four having disappeared with the ravages of time that spanned a great depression and two world wars. From the standpoint of design, engineering, history, culture, and racing, Black Bess stands apart.

BUGATTI TYPE 18
SPORTS TWO-SEATER

Engine:	5-liter, 4-cylinder	Chassis no.:	474
Horse Power:	100	Engine no.:	474

Coachwork by Labourdette. 1 of 3 extant. Former owners include Roland Garros, Louis Coatalen, and Ivy Cummings.

Sold at Bonhams Retromobile Sale, Paris, February 2009, for €2,427,500.

1929
BUGATTI *TYPE 43*
GRAND SPORT

The torpedo profile was sleek and together with its louvered sides and open top seemed to scream speed. It is hardly surprising that Type 43 was immensely successful in sports car racing.

B y the early 1930s Ettore Bugatti had established an unrivalled reputation for building cars with outstanding performance on road or track. The world's greatest racing drivers were enjoying countless successes in the Molsheim factory's products and often choose them for their everyday transport as well.

The foundation of Bugatti's considerable repute was his family of eight-cylinder cars, the first of which, the Type 30, appeared in 1922. The Type 30 shared its chassis, axles, and gearbox with the earlier four-cylinder Type 13 Brescia model, but was powered by an inline eight displacing 1991 cc. Developments of this superb eight-cylinder

engine, with its single overhead camshaft and three valves per cylinder, would go on to power the Type 35 Grand Prix, the Type 38 tourer and Type 43 sports car.

Introduced in 1927, the Type 43 was, in essence, a road-going version of Bugatti's most successful Grand Prix racing car: the Type 35—winner of over 1,000 races, including the Targa Florio, French GP, Italian GP, Spanish GP, German GP, Monaco GP, Czechoslovakian GP, and Belgian GP. It was utterly unassailable.

The Type 43 used the 2260 cc engine, complete with Roots supercharger, introduced on the Type 35B, which was installed in a new chassis similar to that of the Grand Prix racer. Aluminum-cast Type 35 wheels were used, together with the larger radiator and brakes found on the Type 38. The torpedo profile was sleek and together with its louvered sides and open top seemed to scream speed.

Additionally, this particular example had its chassis shortened by its then Dutch owner to make it a pure two-seater, thereby increasing its sporting profile even more. Not surprisingly, considering its Grand Prix derivation, the Type 43 proved immensely successful in sports car racing, being campaigned by the factory and a host of private owners.

Straight off the showroom floor the Type 43 could easily exceed 100 mph and was regarded as the first production car with such capability. When most production sports cars of the era could hit perhaps 80 mph, the Type 43 was a phenomenon.

When it debuted, *Autocar* correspondent W.F. Bradley said of the Type 43: "This model has all the characteristics of a racing car, and is indeed a racing car with a touring body; it looks fast, and it really is fast, but six months' experience with one on French highways has proved that it is one of the safest cars a motorist could handle. Its maximum speed is about 112 mph...its gear ratio and the size of tire used give 20.5 mph per 1000 rpm... one soon becomes satisfied with the knowledge that the car is one of the fastest on the road, and the greatest pleasure is obtained not in attempting to obtain the maximum from

it (that is all but impossible except on a track), but in its wonderful acceleration, its high degree of flexibility, and its remarkable steadiness at all speeds, and particularly when one is negotiating winding hills."

And even with the benefit of hindsight, leading Bugatti expert Hugh Conway later called the Type 43 "one of the four really great Bugatti models" of all.

BUGATTI TYPE 43
GRAND SPORT

Engine:	2.26-liter, 8-cylinder	**Chassis no.:**	43303
Horsepower:	120	**Engine no.:**	130

Coachwork by Bugatti. The world's first 100 mph production car.

Sold at Bonhams Retromobile Sale, Paris, February 2008, for €1,327,500.

1929
BENTLEY
4.5-LITER SUPERCHARGED
SINGLE-SEAT PROTOTYPE

Combining his "Bentley Boy"
high-society image with a fearless
driving talent, he was celebrated
as a style icon and national figure.

Among all the Brooklands habitués of the 1920s and 1930s perhaps the most glamorous and charismatic of all the celebrity pilots was the diminutive Bentley driving Baronet, Sir Henry Ralph Stanley "Tim" Birkin.

Combining his "Bentley Boy" high-society image with a fearless driving talent, he was celebrated as a style icon and national figure. Rakish, daring, and impeccably mannered with appropriate lapses of playboy character, the militarily-mustachioed, be-goggled figure in his neat wind cap and trademark silk polka-dot scarf fluttering in the slipstream personified the English ideal for generations of British motoring enthusiasts.

In truth, Birkin embodied far more than mere celebrity flirting with motor racing. He was intensely competitive, a born sportsman who relished racing for racing's sake, dedicated to maximizing his chances on the track and committed whole-heartedly to making the most of whatever natural talent he possessed. And as one of motoring history's most alluring figures, the car eternally identified with Birkin is this supercharged (or "blower") model.

Having achieved victory in a Bentley at the 24 Hours of Le Mans in 1929 with co-driver Woolf Barnato, Birkin set out to create an ever better champion. He was convinced the secret lay in a lighter-weight car boosted by a supercharger. Interestingly, the model of Bentley that is today the most iconic and sought after—the Blower—was totally resisted by company founder W.O. Bentley.

W.O.'s refusal to accommodate Birkin forced "Tiger Tim" to charge forward independently. With the help of Bentley engineer Clive Gallop, supercharger specialist Amherst

Villiers, and financial backing from heiress Dorothy Paget, this prototype Bentley Blower No. 1 was created.

Once complete, and demonstrating impressive numbers—primarily the enormous increase in horsepower from 130 to 242 in comparison to the standard 4.5-liter racing car, which made it even more powerful than the larger 6.5-liter Bentley—Birkin then convinced Barnato, an investor in Bentley Motors, to persuade (or force, depending on one's perspective) W.O. to build the mandatory 50 commercial Blower models needed in order to qualify for Le Mans. Thus, one of the most fabled motorcars in British history was born.

W.O.'s resistance lay in the belief that increasing displacement was always preferable to forced induction and that "to supercharge a Bentley engine was to pervert its design and corrupt its performance." While he greatly admired Birkin and called him "the greatest Briton of his time," W.O. lamented that he "had a constant urge to do the dramatic thing, a characteristic which I suppose had originally brought him into racing…and his gaily vivid, restless personality seemed to be always driving him on to something new and spectacular, and unfortunately our 4.5-liter car was one of his targets."

While the specifications of the Blower were impressive, the results at Le Mans—the car's raison d'être—and other races were not. Nevertheless, the undeterred Birkin carried on and eventually achieved glowing success in No. 1 at Brooklands, including winning several races and setting a new track record at a blistering 137.96 mph (222 kph).

W.O.'s resistance lay in the belief that increasing displacement was always preferable to forced induction and that "to supercharge a Bentley engine was to pervert its design and corrupt its performance."

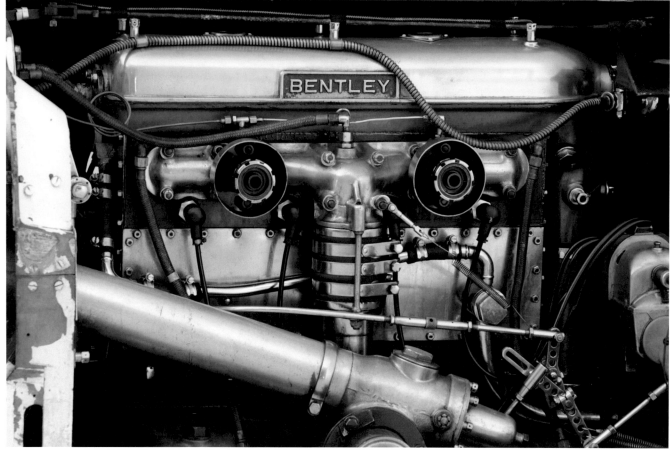

As the first of what would become a car of legendary stature—in automotive history, British identity, and popular culture (*James Bond's* first car, as endowed by author Ian Fleming, was a 1930 4.5-liter Bentley with Amherst Villiers supercharger)—not to mention its competitive victories, this Bentley Blower No. 1 is truly a treasure whose importance cannot be underscored enough.

BENTLEY 4.5-LITER SUPERCHARGED
SINGLE-SEAT PROTOTYPE

Engine:	4.5-liter, 4-cylinder	Chassis no.:	HB 3402
Horse Power:	242	Engine no.:	SM 3901

Sir Henry "Tim" Birkin's "Bentley Blower No. 1" Brooklands record setter.

Sold at Bonhams Goodwood Festival of Speed Sale, Chichester, June 2012 for £5,041,500—a new world auction record for any British car.

1931
ALFA ROMEO
6C 1750
SUPERCHARGED
GRAN SPORT SPIDER

"The 1750, and for that matter the 1500…
must be among the finest ever made
both from the point of view of engineering
and driver satisfaction."

– *M. Frostick, Alfa Romeo–Milano*

It was in 1923 that Enzo Ferrari persuaded Vittorio Jano to leave FIAT's racing department and join him at Alfa Romeo. One of the most gifted and influential automobile engineers of all time, Jano would not only supervise Alfa Romeo's Grand Prix racing program but also design its road cars. This happy state of affairs resulted in the latter emerging as some of the most exciting automobiles of their day, establishing the Milanese marque's reputation for producing sporting driver's cars second to none.

A logical evolution of the Alfa Romeo 6C 1500, itself directly descended from Jano's all-conquering Alfa Romeo P2 that won the World Championship in 1925, the 6C 1750 arrived in 1929 boasting a derivative of the 1500's 6-cylinder engine, enlarged to 1752 cc, thereby providing the model's nomenclature. Constructed in single-cam Turismo and twin-cam Sport (later renamed Gran Turismo) variants,

the 6C 1750 was an exciting, fast sports car combining light weight with sparkling performance. The chassis, also a product of Jano, was low and light, featuring semi-elliptical springs that passed through the front axle. The 6C 1750 would go on to beat much larger and more powerful machinery, the triumph of balance, quickness, and almost thought-control responsiveness over ponderous leviathans.

The 1750's sporting career, aided by its mechanical longevity, extended far beyond its production, amassing countless wins including 1-2-3 finishes in the Mille Miglia and top results at Targa Florio, the Tourist Trophy, and Spa 24 Hours in 1930. Tazio Nuvolari, Attilio Marinoni, Giuseppe Campari, and Achille Varzi—some of the greatest drivers in history—all recorded successes in Jano's "light car" and the model is, quite simply, legendary.

Adding to the appeal of this car is its bodywork by famed coachbuilder Zagato. Nearly a century old, Carrozzeria Zagato has rightfully earned its existence as one of very few surviving coach-building houses. That it has persisted where others did not can almost certainly be attributed to the fact that its designs have always been fresh, different, and of the very finest quality. And in what may be the ultimate expression of life imitating art, even today, founder Ugo Zagato's name sounds exciting, edgy, and modern. Pioneering designs such as the solution to increase localized headroom by creating twin roof bulges, which brought the expression "Double Bubble" into existence, Zagato is a rare example of a coachbuilder creating a hallmark that extends beyond the car brand.

While other coachbuilding houses also created incredible designs for various car manufacturers, today Zagato's work is amongst the most prized. And it is never more so than when one considers pre-Second World War Alfa Romeos and the 1750 model in particular.

Amazingly, the Italian company was quite young when these coveted cars were built, and similar to Gabriel Voisin of Avions Voisin, Zagato's skills had been acquired while building fighter aircraft for his country's air force. By transferring these principles to road-going machinery, he created automobile bodies that were as light and aerodynamic as they were beautiful.

Zagato's attention to detail was legendary, his bodies were costly, and when a wealthy Milanese family took Zagato to court on the grounds that their son had been "mad" to order a "shockingly expensive" Zagato-bodied 8C 2300 Alfa Romeo, the judge rejected their claim on the grounds that "the search for beauty is a most normal thing in a man."

The meticulous approach of Zagato was highly appreciated by the top drivers of the 1920s, and his circle of friends included Giuseppe Campari, Baconin Borzacchini, Giulio Ramponi, and, most notably, Enzo Ferrari who would very clearly link his Alfa successes to Zagato. In later years Ferrari recalled: "Think of how much motoring history was made in those Zagato spiders, first on the RL, then on the 1500 and 1750. It was a glorious series, the fruit of an avant-garde mechanism and a brilliant improvisation that lasted for years and brought so many victories."

As Alfa Romeo refined their 6C 1750 with systematic improvements in each new series, Ugo Zagato raised his

"The search for beauty is a most normal thing in a man."

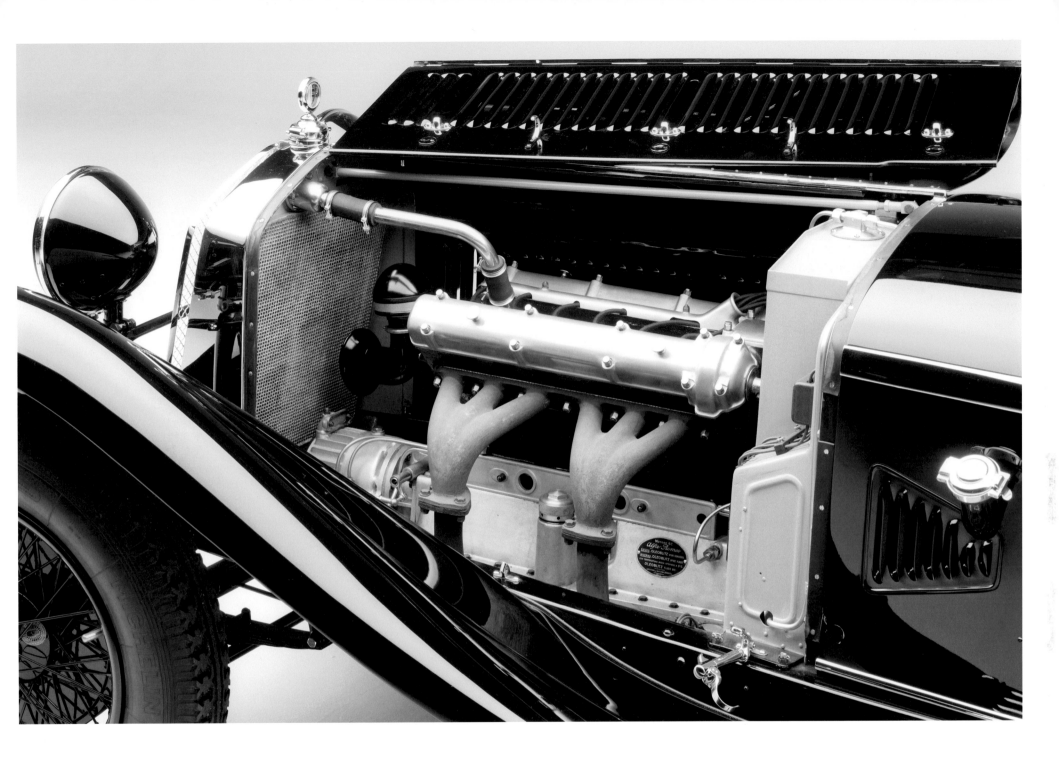

game with refinements in detail and design. Today, it is generally agreed that the zenith of this legendary partnership is what is referred to as the "5th Series" or the fifth iteration in the evolution of the 6C 1750 model. And close inspection of a pure unfettered Zagato body shows just how beautifully crafted these were, with lightness and sleek fluidity incorporated into every aspect from headlight mounts to the intricate windshield, to the sleek way in which the top mechanism rests—manifest evidence of a truly astounding machine.

In the world of car collecting there are four primary criteria that establish a vehicle's worthiness: authenticity, provenance, aesthetics, and engineering. This exceptional Alfa Romeo resoundingly checks all of these boxes.

The history of this particular example, chassis number 10814356, begins in 1931. According to Angela Cherrett's book *Tipo 6C*, 10814356 was completed as a fifth series Gran Sport Spider, featuring the uprated 1752 cc supercharged dual-overhead cam, all-aluminum engine, an improved braking system, and more refined Zagato coach-

work than its predecessors. The new Gran Sport Spider was equipped with engine number 10814356 and fitted with Zagato body number 987.

The first owner of this beautiful machine was Baron Philippe de Gunzbourg who exported it to France and registered it in the village of Saint-Varent in Poitou-Charentes.

A distinguished young man with a taste for fast, sporting motorcars and airplanes and naturally a connoisseur of the finer things in life, the Baron was just 27 years old when he took delivery of his Alfa.

The de Gunzbourgs were a wealthy Russian family with a background in banking and real estate, having moved to France around the turn of the century. Philippe's grandfather, Baron Horace de Gunzbourg, had achieved a tremendous coup when he took a founding interest, along with the Rothschild family, in the Royal Dutch Shell oil company. Philippe therefore grew up with the available means to explore nearly everything he put his mind to, and aviation and motor racing became his preferred interests during the 1920s and 1930s making him the envy of many a man of the period.

The lithe and sporting Alfa Zagato Spider must have been a perfect fit for this gentleman driver. Although not confirmed, it is believed that the Baron was driving this very car when he took first place honors in the 2000 cc class at the La Mothe Sainte Heraye Hill Climb on June 5th, 1932 and again on June 12th at the Puymoyen Hill Climb. De Gunzbourg's best racing result was achieved the following year when he—along with legendary racing driver and Ferrari importer Luigi Chinetti—piloted another Alfa Romeo, an 8C 2300, to a second place finish at the 24 Hours of Le Mans.

When the Second World War broke out across Europe, the de Gunzbourgs, a Jewish family, feared prosecution by the Nazis, and so the Baron sent his wife and son to Switzerland for refuge while he stayed behind in France. Joining the French arm of the British Special Operations Executive, he worked closely with French resistance groups around southwestern France under the aliases Philbert and Edgard. Fortunately, the Baron avoided being captured by the Nazis and was later honored by the de Gaulle government who named the town square in the village of Bergerac after him.

A couple years before the outbreak of war, the dashing and adventurous Baron Philippe de Gunzbourg sold his accomplished Alfa Romeo, whereupon it passed through the ownership of a variety of French enthusiasts, including racer Victor Polledry and a fashion designer from the house of Courrèges.

Over 70 years after de Gunzbourg first relinquished stewardship of the car, and still in a near untouched state of complete originality, the Alfa was bought by an American collector in 2007. Although incredibly well preserved, the car was nonetheless in need of restoration—one that took extra special consideration to preserve the car's remarkably authentic condition.

To ensure absolute accuracy, the world's foremost Alfa Romeo historians and experts were consulted for advice

In the world of car collecting, there are four primary criteria that establish a vehicle's worthiness: authenticity, provenance, aesthetics and engineering.

and guidance throughout the painstaking restoration process. Five years, two American owners, and more than half a million dollars later, the car was completed and restored to its original glory.

Soon thereafter the immaculate convertible sports car was invited to participate in two prestigious 2012 events: the Pebble Beach Concours d'Elegance in California and the Amelia Island Concours d'Elegance in Florida, where it was awarded Best in Class. More importantly, in the spring of 2013 the car proved its roadworthiness and successfully competed in the storied Mille Miglia. Performing faultlessly on this thousand-mile rally in its native Italy, the Alfa—a symbol of Italian national pride and engineering excellence—received an ecstatic reception from local spectators, recalling the 1930 and 1931 editions of the Mille Miglia when Nuvolari and Guidotti, and later Campari and Marinoni, piloted a 6C 1750 Gran Sport Zagato Spider to victory.

After the 2013 Mille Miglia, the car returned to the concours circuit once more when it was selected as one of just 50 automobiles for the exclusive Concorso d'Eleganza Villa d'Este held on the breathtaking shores of Lake Como.

ALFA ROMEO 6C 1750
SUPERCHARGED GRAN SPORT SPIDER

Engine:	1.75-liter, 6-cylinder	**Chassis no.:**	10814356
Horsepower:	85	**Engine no.:**	10814356

Coachwork by Zagato. Formerly owned by Baron Philippe de Gunzbourg and Victor Polledry. Entrant in the Mille Miglia Storica, Pebble Beach Concours d'Elegance, Amelia Island Concours d'Elegance, and Concorso d'Eleganza Villa d'Este.

Sold at Bonhams Scottsdale Auction, Scottsdale, January 2014, for $3,080,000—a world auction record for the model.

1931
INVICTA *S-TYPE*
4.5-LITER LOW CHASSIS FACTORY SPORTS RACER

*Its greatest appeal was its ability
to cover a substantial mileage
at high average speeds with no strain,
either to driver or the machinery.*

In an era when most cars stood tall, the 4.5-liter S-Type Invicta, with its dramatically underslung chassis, caused a sensation and few sports cars before or since have so looked the part.

The Invicta Company's origins go back to 1924, when motoring veterans Noel Macklin and Oliver Lyle got together to create a car combining American levels of flexibility and performance with European quality and roadholding.

Like the contemporary Bentley, the Invicta was designed by men with a personal background in competition motoring, and both were produced to an exemplary standard. Price was only a secondary consideration, a factor that contributed largely to both firms' failure to weather the Great Depression of the 1930s. Like Bentley, Invicta struggled against rising costs and falling sales, the final car leaving the factory appropriately enough on Friday the 13th of October 1933, although a handful of cars were assembled at the company's service depot in Chelsea up to 1936. In total, it is estimated that only 1,000 Invictas of all types were made, making representations of the marque today quite uncommon.

Apart from a handful of prototypes built at Macklin's home in Surrey, all Invictas were powered by the tireless six-cylinder engines made by Henry Meadows. Invicta cars quickly established a reputation for outstanding durability, which was underlined by the award of the Royal Automobile Club's (RAC) coveted Dewar Trophy in 1926 and 1929, largely for the marque's success in long-distance reliability trials, including the astounding around-the-world trip by lady drivers Violette Cordery and Eleanor Simpson.

Launched at the 1930 Motor Show at Olympia, the S-type featured a new underslung chassis that achieved a much lower center of gravity by positioning the axles above the frame rails instead of below, as was normal practice at the time. Just about the only thing the S-Type Invicta had in common with its contemporary stablemates was the 4.5-liter Meadows engine, which was also used for

the NLC and A models. Like most low-revving engines, it delivered ample torque in the lower and middle speed ranges. In fact, the Invicta could be throttled down to 6–8 mph in top gear—despite its relatively high 3.6:1 final drive ratio—and could then accelerate rapidly and without complaint when the accelerator was depressed. Contemporary motoring press reports typically recorded acceleration figures of 10–70 mph in 19 seconds, which speaks volumes for the Invicta's legendary flexibility.

Invicta's standard cars had an impressive top speed of 95 mph, with more to come in racing trim. However, the purpose of the S-Type was not speed at all costs, rather a

> *"The low chassis Invicta was probably the best-looking sports car in the vintage tradition ever to be produced in England. I can think of no contemporary unsupercharged motorcar of similar capacity, made here, which could outperform it—and very few built elsewhere…"*
>
> – JR Buckley, *The 4½-Liter S-Type Invicta*

fast but comfortable high-speed touring car. And though it met with moderate success in racing in the hands of private owners in the early 1930s, its greatest appeal was its ability to cover a substantial mileage at high average speeds with no strain, either to driver or the machinery.

With Invicta's reputation for sterling reliability cemented by the success of the Cordery/Simpson feat just two years earlier in a 3-liter Invicta, it was not considered necessary to prove the 4.5-liter S-Type. As such, upon its debut, the company took the S-Type straight into competition by entering the most challenging long-distance trials and achieving notable successes in, for example, the Austrian Alpine Trial and twice winning a Coupe des Glaciers under Donald Healey in addition to the 1931 Monte Carlo Rally. Later, an S-Type also took the International Sports Car Record at Shelsley Walsh Hill Climb and, by way of variety, the Mountain Circuit lap record at Brooklands in 1931 and again in 1932, courtesy of Raymond Mays.

This particular car was raced by the factory in a number of contests, including the Brooklands Double Twelve, the Irish Tourist Trophy, and the Brooklands Long Mountain Handicap of 1931, winning the latter. Later, once in private hands, it was campaigned further at Brooklands, Silverstone, Goodwood, and the Prescott Hill Climb. Still retaining its glorious original condition, this charger is a sight to behold.

Admired for its exceptional driving abilities and iconic Pre-Second World War British style—indeed the car that inspired the legendary (Jaguar) SS 100 of nearly a decade later—the Invicta S-Type is a motorcar which surely deserves a greater share of the spotlight.

INVICTA S-TYPE 4.5-LITER
LOW CHASSIS FACTORY SPORTS RACER

Coachwork by Cadogan. Raced in the Irish Tourist Trophy, at Brooklands, Goodwood, and Silverstone.

Engine: 4.5-liter, 6-cylinder   **Chassis no.:** S39

Horsepower: 110

Sold at Bonhams Goodwood Revival Sale, Chichester, September 2013 for £953,500—a world auction record for the marque.

ALFA ROMEO
8C 2300

SUPERCHARGED SPIDER
LUNGO FACTORY RACER

" ...It's a wonderful car for racing, lightweight, very fast, 130 mph ..."

Few great classic sports cars can match the intense sensory overload provided by the supreme Alfa Romeo 8C 2300. From visual, auditory, olfactory, and tactile senses, the mix is lusty and unforgettable. Add to that the historical provenance of leading races of the day and leading figures of the day, and the combination is an automobile of no meager stature.

This great car was first registered by the Alfa Romeo company on June 3rd, 1932 and just two weeks later became the third of Alfa Romeo's 1932 factory-entered 24 Hours of Le Mans cars. In preparation for the world's most prestigious race, the car was bodied by Touring coach-builders of Milan and featured a different windshield and more robust front wing stays than the two other factory team race cars.

Carrying the race number 9, it was co-driven by the highly capable, intensely competitive British aristocrats Sir Henry "Tim" Birkin and Francis Curzon Earl Howe, who, with the withdrawal from racing that year by Bentley, eagerly joined team Alfa Romeo for a chance at the Le Mans prize. Unfortunately, while the English duo ran fast and strong and led the 25 starters for a time at that year's Le Mans, No. 9 was forced to retire with a thrown rod, thus dashing any hope for victory.

Taken across the channel to England for repairs at Birkin's "Blower Bentley" facilities, the car was then entered in the Royal Automobile Club (RAC) Tourist Trophy at Ards, Northern Ireland, with Howe at the wheel. Impressively, he finished the 410-mile race with the fastest time, but with the RAC handicap system only officially placed fourth, with Birkin coming in fifth in another Alfa Romeo 8C 2300.

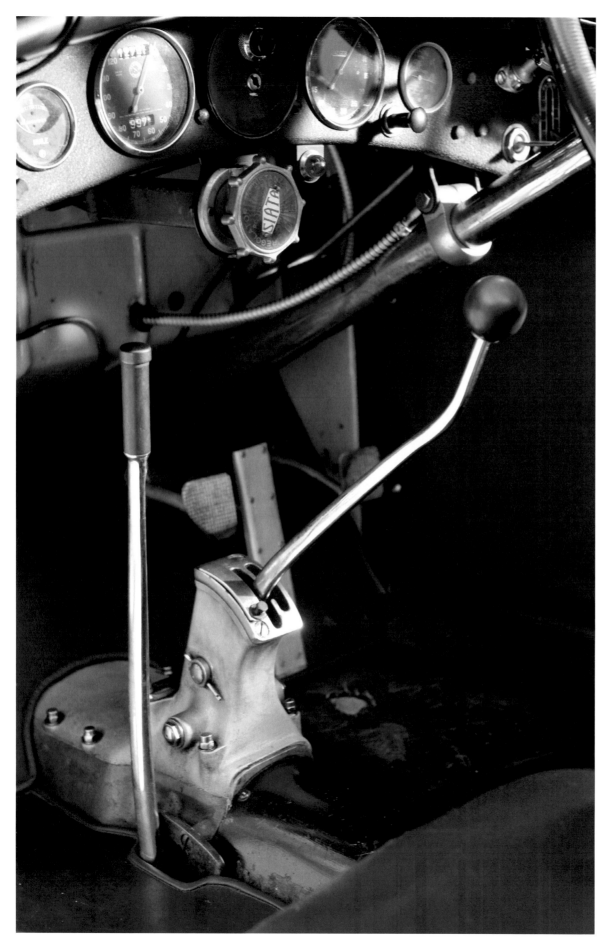

This great car became the third of Alfa Romeo's 1932 factory–entered 24 Hours of Le Mans cars.

After what might be interpreted as a moral victory, the car was returned to Alfa Romeo in Italy, whereupon the factory sold it to famed racing champion and opera singer Giuseppe Campari, winner of the Italian GP, French GP, Mille Miglia, and many more.

In Campari's care the car was consigned to Pinin Farina coachbuilders of Turin to be rebodied from its touring-made racing regulation form to a road-useable roadster. Shortly thereafter, the car was sold to Italo Balbo—the decorated First World War hero, Marshal of the fascist-era Italian Air Force, Governor-General of Tripolitania (Italian Libya), and man for whom Balbo Drive in Chicago is named.

After the death of Balbo—the result of a friendly fire incident in Tobruk—the car changed hands a number of times until it came into the stewardship of renowned horologist and motorcar collector George Daniels in England.

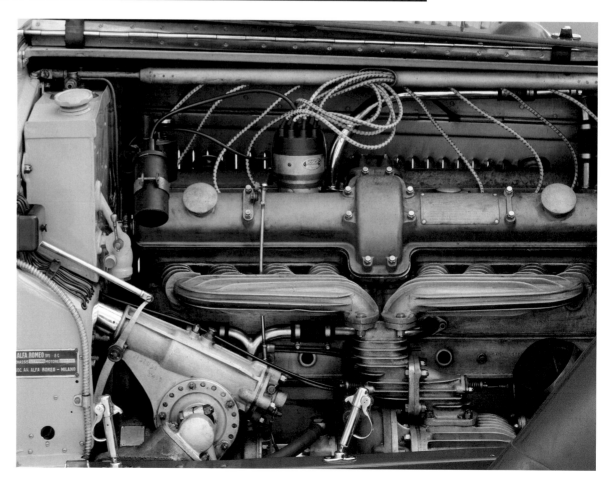

Daniels, wanting the factory-specified body back on the car, both for the purpose of historical accuracy and for racing, commissioned Jolley coachbuilders to rebody the vehicle back into the Le Mans-specification form in which it appears today. Delighted with the car in every respect, Daniels remarked, in his typical, understated manner, "...It's a wonderful car for racing, lightweight, very fast, 130 mph, and it fulfills all my needs for a sports racing car."

Clinching two first-in-class finishes as well as a second in the Manx Classic, the car demonstrated—nearly 70 years after its debut—that it has lost none of its capabilities.

ALFA ROMEO 8C 2300
SUPERCHARGED SPIDER LUNGO FACTORY RACER

| Engine: | 2336 cc, 8-cylinder | Chassis no.: | 2211065 |
| Horsepower: | 150 | Engine no.: | 2211065 |

Coachwork by Touring, Pinin Farina and Jolley. Raced by Sir Henry "Tim" Birkin and Francis Curzon Earl Howe in the 24 Hours of Le Mans and RAC Tourist Trophy; owned by racing champion Giuseppe Campari and Italian hero Italo Balbo.

Sold at Bonhams Goodwood Festival of Speed Sale, Chichester, June 2012, for £2,689,500—a world auction record for the model.

1935
ALFA ROMEO *8C 35*
SUPERCHARGED GRAND PRIX
RACING MONOPOSTO

Roaring onto the track, Nuvolari
took full advantage of both the circuit and
the 8C, and soon ripped into Auto Union's
lead against their colossal V16s.

Faced with competing against the enormous might of the German state-backed Auto Union C-Type and Mercedes-Benz W25E "Silver Arrow" cars, Alfa Romeo knew that to defend its stronghold on racing its contender would need to be very special.

The answer from their gifted designer, Vittorio Jano, was this first all-independently suspended, big-engined Grand Prix racer known as the Tipo 8C 35 Monoposto. The single-seat, open-wheeled, supercharged bullet was a force of mechanical design, although it soon proved not enough to match the massively powered German cars on the faster tracks. However, on the tighter circuits it was able to gain a distinct advantage.

The most famous victory of all was in Livorno in August 1936 at the Coppa Ciano with none other than Tazio

Nuvolari. Under the banner of Scuderia Ferrari, the latest Alfa Romeo V12 models, the Tipo 12C 36, were fielded. However, Nuvolari's car failed at the start, and after a long delay in the pits the gifted driver, growing ever more anxious, insisted on taking over teammate Carlo Pintacuda's 8C 35.

Roaring onto the track, Nuvolari took full advantage of both the circuit and the comparatively lithe 8C and soon ripped into rival Auto Union's lead against their colossal V16s. With Auto Union driver Hans Stuck already sidelined, the remaining two Auto Unions, piloted by Bernd Rosemeyer and Achille Varza, pushed hard against Nuvolari's intensifying pressure but finally broke down. Thus, the "Flying Mantuan," astonishing all in attendance, won outright and led Alfa Romeo to a full podium sweep.

Immediately after the finish, the Scuderia Ferrari pit crew saw Rosemeyer striding towards them. Expecting a

verbal assault because Nuvolari had barged the German's tail during his pursuit, the crew braced themselves. Instead, the gracious Rosemeyer had simply come to praise Nuvolari, calling him *Il Mago*, "The Magician."

Although two contemporary British periodicals, *The Autocar* and *Speed,* both attributed this very car, chassis no. 50013, as being the car in which Nuvolari stunningly won the Coppa Ciano, records cannot definitively prove nor disprove this. Nevertheless, under the ownership of its subsequent owner, this car did go on to claim several more impressive victories.

At the end of summer in 1936, Scuderia Ferrari sold the car to Swiss privateer Hans Ruesch. Immediately the young Swissman entered it in the Donington GP and, with co-driver RJB "Dick" Seaman, won first place. Next was the Mountain Championship at Brooklands in which he took second, followed by the fastest time at the January

1937 Rand GP near Johannesburg, although the handicap system officially placed him in fourth. Back in Europe, Ruesch won no fewer than seven events, including the Finnish GP, Romanian GP, Swiss GP, GP des Frontieres in Belgium, and the Mountain Championship at Brooklands, not to mention setting a new standing start record at Montlhery. Ruesch and the Nuvolari-attributed Alfa 8C were a force to be reckoned with.

In 1938 the International Grand Prix Formula was changed and limited supercharged engines to no more than 3-liters, making this 3.8-liter racer ineligible. Ruesch then focused on non-GP events in Britain, achieving podium placements in the Sydenham Trophy and Shelsley Walsh Hill Climb—competitions that were highly respectable to be sure but far from the prestige of Grand Prix. Finally, as a fitting finale for Ruesch and the Italian charger that brought him so much success, he set what would become the perpetual Brooklands Campbell Circuit lap record for the 3 to 5-liter category.

Under the ownership of Dennis Poore, the car continued to be raced in a number of events, including winning the 1947 Grandsen Trophy and the 1950 Royal Automobile Club Hill Climb Championship. Even more fitting, Poore won the Vintage Sports Car Club Seaman Trophy three times—named in memory of Dick Seaman, who died leading the 1939 Belgium GP at Spa for team Mercedes-Benz, and who himself helped clinch victory at Donington in this very car. In 1955, the race car was retired effectively for good and sat entombed in storage for several decades.

In the late 1990s, the car, after having been exhumed, underwent a thorough and historically accurate restoration by its then new owner and, under its most recent owner, was reunited with the track, being campaigned at

Donington, Mugello, Goodwood, Lime Rock, Sonoma, and Laguna Seca among others, where it frequently won its class. No mere static display, this 80-year old racer still has what it takes.

From its Scuderia Ferrari roots, Nuvolari-associated victory, multiple Ruesch championships and Poore titles, this is not only the finest surviving mid-1930s Alfa Romeo 8C 35 but also one of the most historic pre-war cars extant.

ALFA ROMEO 8C 35 SUPERCHARGED
GRAND PRIX RACING MONOPOSTO

Engine:	3822 cc, 8-cylinder	Chassis no.:	50013
Horsepower:	330	Engine no.:	50013

Raced by Tazio Nuvolari (attributed), Dick Seaman, Hans Ruesch, and Dennis Poore. Winner of the Donington GP, Finnish GP, Romanian GP, Swiss GP, and more.

Sold at Bonhams Goodwood Revival Sale, Chichester, September 2013, for £5,937,500—a world auction record for the marque.

1936
LAGONDA *LG45R*
RAPIDE SPORTS-RACING
TWO-SEATER

Heralding from a time when there were truly "all-rounders," the LG45R is fast, comfortable, uncomplicated, and rakishly handsome.

From the halcyon days of pre-war sports racing comes what author and marque expert Geoff Seaton calls "the most famous Lagonda of all."

Heralding from a time when there were truly "all-rounders"—cars that with a few minor modifications could be campaigned in all manner of events: LG45R is fast, comfortable, uncomplicated to drive, and rakishly handsome.

Founded in England in 1906, by an American boat and motorcycle builder named Wilber Gunn, who named the company after a creek in his native Ohio, Lagonda first grabbed international headlines when its Torpedo model won the 1910 Moscow-Saint Petersburg race.

Although competitive and of good build quality, it would be years before Lagonda became established as a true sporting marque. Then, at the height of the Great Depression, it achieved its greatest triumph—winning the 24 Hours of Le Mans in 1935.

Notwithstanding this victory, financial troubles prevailed and the end seemed inevitable until businessman Alan Good rescued the company that same year.

Good's first order of business was hiring W.O. Bentley away from Rolls-Royce. Immediately, Bentley, as chief designer, took Lagonda into the luxury car market with the LG45 model. With a number of improvements, including modifications to the Le Mans-winning Meadows engine, Lagonda had an all-new and very impressive line-up for the 1936 London Motor Show.

Longtime Lagonda associates Arthur Fox and Bob Nicholl had been preparing and racing Lagonda cars as early as 1927 and, with support from the company, became its quasi-factory racing team. Similar to Enzo Ferrari and his private Scuderia Ferrari (acting as the quasi-factory Alfa Romeo team), Fox and Nicholl were representing the Lagonda's vital interests in motor racing circuits.

In 1936, Lagonda built two two-seater competition cars specifically for Fox and Nicholl to compete in the 24 Hours of Le Mans (this car being one of them).

"The most famous
Lagonda of all."

– Geoff Seaton

Unfortunately, that year's race was cancelled due to strikes in France. So, Fox and Nicholl entered the cars in the French Grand Prix, known at the time as the Grand Prix de l'Automobile Club de France, with this one, chassis number 12111, being driven by Algerian-born French driver Marcel Lehoux. While Lehoux was forced to retire early, the other Fox and Nicholl Lagonda handily won its class.

Next, number 12111 was entered in the Royal Automobile Club (RAC) Tourist Trophy at Ards with aristocratic driver Brian Lewis (later Lord Essendon) at the wheel. Running strong and in second place after two hours, the car slid off the road and struck a bank. Lewis rejoined the race and recovered to run an epic duel for third place with Eddie Hall in his famous Derby Bentley. Sadly, after four hours, Lewis was forced to retire due to loss of oil from a broken stud in the engine timing cover.

Impressively, however, Lewis' fastest lap of the Ards circuit during his fight back through the field was achieved at a shattering 83.20 mph, compared to Hall's fastest of 81.07 mph. If one can imagine maintaining such an average speed around a narrow, undulating, winding loop of Ulster roads through villages, a town center, and out around the rolling farmland of Northern Ireland, one can understand the remarkable performance of the Lagonda LG45R Rapide in capable hands.

Undeterred, in fact likely encouraged, Fox and Nicholl next entered the car in the British Racing Driver's Club 500 Miles at Brooklands, with former Le Mans winner Francis Curzon partnering with Lewis as co-driver. Drawing on their considerable experience, the duo achieved third place and won a green marble-block trophy that is today awarded annually as the Fox & Nicholl Trophy by the British Vintage Sports Car Club at Silverstone.

In 1937, Fox and Nicholl were finally able to have the car race at Le Mans—wearing the number 3 it is seen with today—but it was forced to retire due to unspecified

mechanical trouble. Unfortunately, the car fared no better at the RAC Tourist Trophy at Donington, when, with Charlie Martin at the wheel, it crashed. Nevertheless, once repaired the car was driven by *Speed* editor Alan Hess to a new record of 104.4 miles covered within one hour from a standing start—and with a passenger to boot!

After the Second World War, and over the following years, the car experienced various owners who maintained its integrity and purpose by campaigning it successfully in club races in Britain, the Mille Miglia Storica in Italy, and at races in America at Laguna Seca and Lime Rock, among others.

W.O. Bentley took Lagonda straight into the luxury car market with the LG45.

Having duly earned its reputation as the most famous Lagonda of all, this enormously charismatic, indefatigable warrior—wearing its 1937 Le Mans Fox and Nicholl livery—is not only still ready for more, but is quite capable of providing it.

LAGONDA LG45R
RAPIDE SPORTS-RACING TWO-SEATER

Coachwork by Fox & Nicholl. Raced in the French GP, 24 Hours of Le Mans, RAC Tourist Trophy, and BRDC 500

Engine:	4.4-liter, 6-cylinder	**Chassis no.:**	12111
Horsepower:	140	**Engine no.:**	12111

Sold at Bonhams Goodwood Revival Sale, Chichester, September 2014, for £1,569,500—a world auction record for the marque.

BUGATTI *TYPE 57S*

ATALANTE COUPE "BARN FIND"

Exclusive and expensive, it was the pinnacle of mid-1930s styling finesse with the added benefit of respectable muscle hidden underneath.

His stable of cars was exotic and extensive, with *Time* magazine purportedly calling it "Europe's most elaborate" collection of racing cars.

It would come at no surprise then, that when choosing his personal road car, Howe would seek out the machine with the highest combination of engineering, performance, refinement, comfort, and style. At the time, there was really only one car in Europe that could fill such a tall order and that was the Bugatti Type 57S. Exclusive and expensive, it was the pinnacle of mid-1930s styling finesse with the added benefit of respectable muscle hidden underneath.

The English aristocrat Francis Curzon, the Fifth Earl Howe secured his place in history with his victory at the 24 Hours of Le Mans in 1931, driving an Alfa Romeo 8C 2300 with co-driver Sir Henry "Tim" Birkin.

In his day, Howe mixed with the famous "Bentley Boys", Barnato, Benjafield, Birkin, and Kidston and was a familiar figure at motoring events. He raced Le Mans a total of six times and competed at many of the major international circuits such as Brooklands, Monaco, and Ulster. In addition to his greatest win—Le Mans—he also won the Donington Park Trophy in 1933 and the Grosvenor Grand Prix in 1938.

Like his good friend and driving partner Birkin, Howe was fiercely competitive but also privileged and mixed with the upper echelons of London's high speed and high fashion society.

Bugatti's standard Type 57 had already earned its credentials, and even though the 57S shared many of its elder sibling's features, the differences were great enough to set the S in a league apart.

The fundamental difference between the two models lay in the frame design, which gave birth to the "S"

Graced with sensuous Art Deco lines and capped with a distinctive V-shaped radiator, the Jean Bugatti–designed automobile was literally a work of mechanical sculpture.

designation. Representing *surbaissé,* or "lowered" in English, the new low-slung frame featured a shorter wheelbase with the rear axle passing directly through the frame, delivering a lower center of gravity, resulting in better handling, while de Ram shock absorbers provided damping cleverly engineered to increase with speed.

Next was the mechanical excellence, which was achieved by fitting a modified crank case with dual oil pumps and dry sump lubrication. High compression pistons gave the new eight-cylinder engine a significant performance edge,

With these credentials, it was little wonder that Howe, a man of means with a penchant for speed and luxury, ordered a bespoke 57S.

with the clutch being reinforced to cope with the extra output. Ignition was by a Scintilla Vertex magneto driven from the left-hand camshaft.

Graced with sensuous Art Deco lines and capped with a distinctive V-shaped radiator, the Jean Bugatti-designed automobile was literally a work of mechanical sculpture.

In 1936, Bugatti fielded a team of specially built Type 57S race cars and won the Grand Prix de l'Automobile Club de France (later known as the French GP), the Grand Prix de la Marne, and the Grand Prix du Comminges. As if that were not enough, they also set new 1-Hour, 6-Hour,

and 24-Hour records at Montlhéry. Then, in 1937, a pair of French drivers, Wimille and Benoist, drove one of these cars to victory at the 24 Hours of Le Mans at an all-time record average speed of 85.125 mph.

With these credentials it was little wonder that Howe, a man of means with a penchant for speed and luxury, ordered a bespoke 57S in 1937.

Approximately seven months later, in May 1937, Howe's Bugatti 57S Atalante Coupe arrived in London.

For several years Howe enjoyed his automobile, taking it to many a race meet and displaying it at events such

as the Eastbourne Concours d'Elegance, until 1945 when, after an accident, the car left Howe's association.

Sometime thereafter it passed in succession to four different owners, none of whom made much use of the car, with the last owner storing it in a locked garage in 1960.

After the owner's death in 2007, the car was discovered by the owner's family sitting exactly as it was left nearly a half-century earlier.

BUGATTI TYPE 57S
ATALANTE COUPE "BARN FIND"

Coachwork by Bugatti. 1 of 17 built.
Formerly owned by Francis Curzon, Fifth Earl Howe.

Engine:	3257 cc, 8-cylinder	Chassis no.:	57502
Horsepower:	135	Engine no.:	26S

Sold at Bonhams Retromobile Sale, Paris, February 2009, for €3,417,500.

1939

TALBOT-LAGO
T150 C SS
AEROCOUPE

It was a banner year for Talbot-Lago...
they took full podium sweeps of first,
second, and third places at the French GP and
Marseilles GP...It was an onslaught that took
the leading contenders by complete surprise.

The story of Talbot-Lago is best appreciated when understanding the background of its Venetian founder Antonio Lago.

Raised among actors, musicians, and government officials, Lago's family was full of creativity, drama, and politics. As a young man he developed relationships with a variety of important people such as Pope John IV and Benito Mussolini. Although a founding member of the Italian National Fascist Party, Lago became very disillusioned with fascism and became a very outspoken critic. As a result, he became a target for the Black Shirts and, being under constant threat, carried a grenade with him at all times. One day while in a small restaurant, three fascist militiamen came to apprehend him. As they entered they shot the proprietor, giving Lago time to pull the pin on his

grenade, toss it, and run out the back door. When he heard that one of the assailants had died, Lago fled to Paris as a fugitive, never to return to Italy.

After earning engineering degrees, Lago worked for aerospace engineers Pratt & Whitney in California, then represented Isotta-Fraschini in England, and later negotiated the rights to license the Wilson pre-selector gearbox—a breakthrough innovation that would soon be adopted in either Wilson form or proprietary variants by Auto Union, Bugatti, Cord, Crossley, Daimler, ERA, Maybach, and others.

In 1935, the Anglo-French automobile company Sunbeam-Talbot-Darracq—with whom Lago was working—was collapsing and, armed with the Wilson transmission license and his own suspensions system, Lago negotiated the purchase of the Talbot arm of the conglomerate.

The next year Lago and his newly named company Talbot-Lago, based in Suresnes, France, decided to competitively run their upgraded T150 C model, made

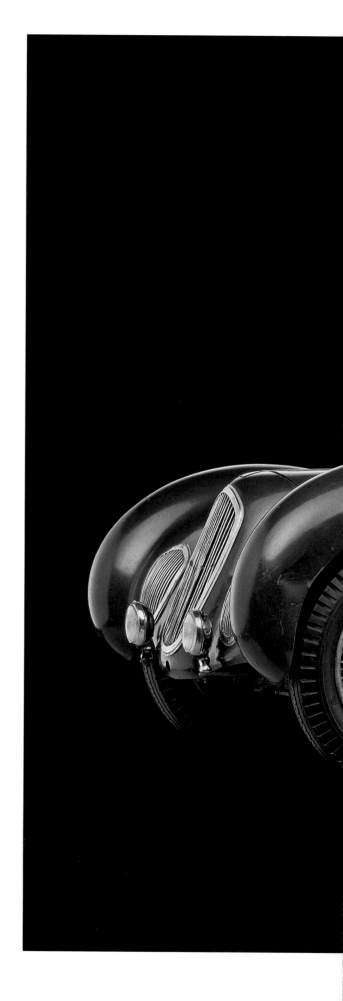

As they entered they shot the proprietor, giving Lago time to pull the pin on his grenade, toss it, and run out the back door.

drastically more powerful by the Walter Brecchia-designed four-cylinder engine. Convincing racing great René Dreyfus to head the factory's race team, the T150 C made an impressive albeit unsuccessful showing at that year's French GP at Montlhéry and garnered the attention of the sporting community.

1937, however, proved to be a banner year for Talbot-Lago, when they took full podium sweeps of first, second, and third places at the French GP as well as the Marseilles GP, first place at the Tunisia GP, first and second places at the RAC Tourist Trophy, second place at the Pau GP, and

second and third places at the Marne GP. It was an onslaught that took leading contenders Alfa Romeo, Bugatti, and Delahaye by complete surprise.

In the midst of this enormous success Talbot-Lago introduced the masterful new T150 C SS, a short wheel-base touring version of the T150 C that had been so victorious. It sported the four-liter, six-cylinder, overhead-valve engine with triple Zenith-Stromberg carburetors matched to a modified version of the Wilson transmission. Boasting 140 horsepower it could cruise all day near 100 mph, making the model's designation — "C" for competition and

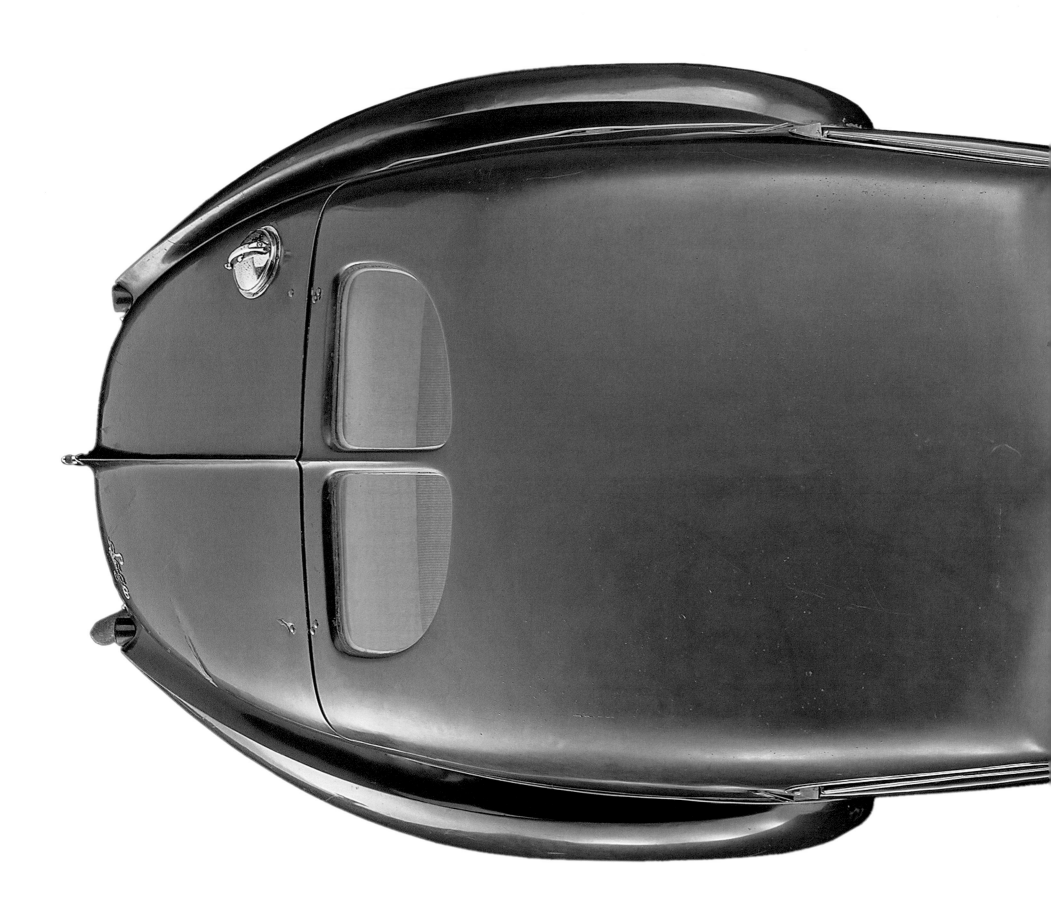

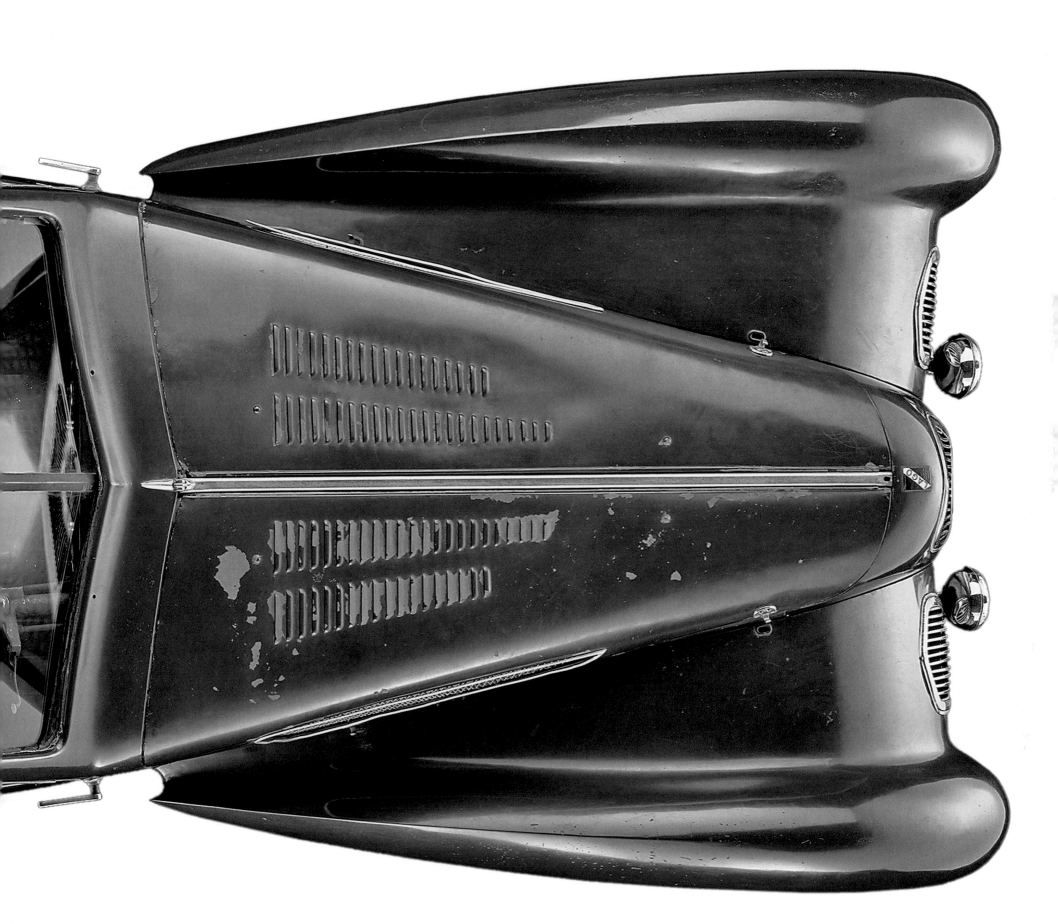

It was sensual and advertised speed even when stationary and, more remarkably, the C SS could generate the velocity exuded by its form.

"SS" for super sport—an accurate descriptor. And belying this power was a voluptuous coachbuilt body designed by Figoni et Falaschi. Nicknamed *goutte d'eau* or "drop of water" in French, and called the "teardrop" in English, it was an ebullient series of curves accentuated by strategic placements of chrome, finished with a dramatic fastback.

The streamlined, elegant, art deco design cloaking a machine of impressive output was a sensation and would soon become regarded by many as Figoni et Falaschi's opus. It was sensual and advertised speed even when stationary, and, more remarkably, the C SS could generate the velocity exuded by its form. In 1938, a standard, off-the-showroom-floor T150 C SS remarkably clinched third at the 24 Hours of Le Mans and then repeated the feat at the Coupe de Paris at Montlhéry.

Less than 30 of these cars were made, most by bodied Figoni et Falaschi. However, there were four special AeroCoupes completed by Carrosserie Pourtout, this car being one of them.

With gifted designer Georges Paulin employed by Marcel Pourtout, the dynamic duo created a design that was very similar to the Figoni et Falaschi teardrop but more aerodynamic, with a less studied look. Just four AeroCoupes were built, each slightly different, with three surviving today and only this one in original, unrestored condition.

The hallmark would be one of Paulin's last designs. During the Second World War, as an active member of the

French resistance, Paulin was found out, captured, and executed by the Nazis in 1942.

In 1950 and 1951, privateer sportsman Pierre Boncompagni, who by then owned this car, campaigned it extensively under his Ecurie Nice team using the *nom de course* "Pagnibon." The Frenchman achieved many victories with the car, including winning his class at Nice, Orleans, Bressuire, Agen, and the Mont Ventoux hill climb.

At some point the car came to America and was left, under the stewardship of its California owner, in long term, unmolested rest until it was brought to light by a member of the owner's family.

Representing a unique, glorious age of handbuilt luxury sports cars, this Talbot-Lago time capsule is not only exceedingly rare but like all great artworks is accomplished and distinct, providing a fascinating window into the minds of its creators.

TALBOT-LAGO T150 C SS
AEROCOUPE

| Engine: | 3996 cc, 6-cylinders | Chassis no.: | 90120 |
| Horsepower: | 140 | Engine no.: | 17318-C |

Coachwork by Pourtout. 1 of 3 extant.

Sold at Bonhams Quail Lodge Auction, Carmel, in August 2008, for $4,847,000—a world record for the marque.

1951
—
1960

1951
FERRARI *212*
EXPORT BERLINETTA

This car represents the earliest roots
and very essence of Ferrari—a competition
car dressed in a Touring body.

More important than its fashionable provenance, however, are two aspects that set this car apart.

This racing-bred V-12 Ferrari was delivered new to Italian tailor and racing driver Augusto Caraceni of the eponymous fashion house. Founded in 1913 by Domenico Caraceni, "The Father of Italian Tailoring," the House of Caraceni made bespoke suits for some of the best dressed and most recognizable men of the twentieth century, including Enzo Ferrari, Gianni Agnelli, Gary Cooper, Aristotle Onassis, and even Yves St. Laurent.

Domenico's son, Augusto Caraceni, steeped in the family business, knew good design when he saw it. So when a car was needed to compete in the 1951 Stella Alpina (in which he would place second), it was this sports racing Ferrari clothed in the legendary Berlinetta body by famous Milanese coachbuilder Touring that was selected by one of the most renowned sartorial names in the world.

First is the serial number. Ferrari implemented the unique process of using odd numbers for road-going chassis and even numbers for their raison d'être—racing and competition chassis. Second is the coachwork. Perhaps Ferrari is most associated with Pinin Farina, but it was Touring that bodied Enzo's very first cars—the two Tipo 815 models built for the Mille Miglia under Auto-Avio Costruzioni. This car, then, represents the earliest roots and very essence of Ferrari—a competition car dressed in a Touring body.

Just four of these even-numbered sports racing models were created in Berlinetta form, which was Touring's first closed racing model built for Ferrari. Using a shorter and more rigid chassis, they received a highly tuned version of Colombo's 212 engine featuring a triple carburetor setup, higher compression, and dry sump lubrication. The

lithe Touring Superleggera Berlinetta bodies had racing features such as Plexiglas windows, quick-release fuel filler, and an interior stripped of most creature comforts. The result was a car nearly 440 lbs. (200 kg) lighter than the road version and historically a very important part of Ferrari's early racing efforts on their road to domination.

The result was a car that is historically a very important part of Ferrari's early racing efforts on their road to domination.

FERRARI 212
EXPORT BERLINETTA

Engine:	2562 cc, 12-cylinder	**Chassis no.:**	0088 E
Horsepower:	170	**Engine no.:**	0088 E

Coachwork by Touring. Formerly owned by Augusto Caraceni.

Sold at Bonhams Scottsdale Auction, Scottsdale, January 2014, for $3,190,000.

1951–1960
ECURIE *ECOSSE* GROUP

As Scotland's first organized motorsports team, they achieved spectacular success by twice winning the ne plus ultra of endurance racing: The 24 Hours of Le Mans.

1951

JAGUAR XK120
ROADSTER

The legendary Ecurie Ecosse (French for Team Scotland) was established by Scotsman David Murray in Edinburgh in 1951. As Scotland's first organized motorsports team, they achieved—quite unexpectedly by most—spectacular success by twice winning the ne plus ultra of endurance racing: the 24 Hours of Le Mans.

One of the most often asked questions is why a French name was used for a Scottish team? The answer is not in the long history shared by France and Scotland as allies against England. Rather, Murray was an admitted Francophile who owned a wine shop featuring French wines. He also reasoned that if he was going to develop a team that would race internationally, having a French title might help attract more starting money from European organizers.

The next most often asked question is how it began its famous association with Jaguar? The Esso oil and petrol company was prepared to sponsor the newly formed team but required that they have three cars, all the same model. Murray owned a Jaguar XK120 which he had sold to local driver Bill Dobson, and the skilled racer from Perthshire, Ian Stewart, also owned an XK120. Then there was Sir James Scott Douglas, a very competent driver who owned an XK120 and happened to be Scottish. And so began Ecurie Ecosse.

In truth, the team would race other marques during its tenure, such as Austin-Healey, Brabham, Connaught, Cooper, and Tojeiro, but it began with Jaguar and it was with Jaguar that they achieved their greatest victories.

As for the famous color, Stewart's XK120 was already Flag Metallic Blue, which was a perfect coincidence since blue was the same base color as the national flag of Scotland. This Jaguar XK120 Roadster, known by its registration number LXO126, is one of the three founding cars

of Ecurie Ecosse, the most successful of that trio, and today the sole survivor.

Upon its racing debut in 1952, Douglas' LXO126 achieved numerous podium placements and/or class finishes with Douglas behind the wheel including at Castle Combe, Charterhall, Curragh, Ibsley, and Isle of Man. Its most important victory, however, was historic third place overall finish in the Reims Grand Prix. With Stirling Moss taking first place in a Jaguar factory-entered C-Type and Douglas in his Ecurie Ecosse-entered XK120, the two podium wins were heralded by the press as a giant triumph for Britain and, in the words of *Autosport*, "will do much to atone for the Le Mans failure" (in which Jaguar did not finish).

The next year Ecurie Ecosse replaced the trio of XK120s with C-Types, so Douglas retained his laurel-laden car as his personal road vehicle. But when one of the C-Types rolled during practice for the 1953 Nürburgring 1000 km, Douglas' XK120 was pressed back into service overnight.

Racing against an international field of over 50 cars, with many of them superior to the XK120, Douglas and co-driver Ninian Sanderson nonetheless finished a highly respectable tenth overall and helped Ecosse teammates Ian Stewart and Roy Salvadori in their C-Type take a remarkable second overall.

Now rightfully recognized as serious challengers and not just hopeful dilettantes, Ecurie Ecosse went on to earn both international and industry respect. The team would count future three-time Formula 1 World Champion Sir Jackie Stewart and his older brother Jimmy among its drivers, and would compete in both sports car classics and Grand Prix racing. In just 10 seasons, Ecurie Ecosse scored some 68 victories, including its legendary twin conquests at Le Mans.

From a humble garage in a cobbled Edinburgh mews, operating invariably upon a shoestring budget, this proudly Scottish blue-liveried team would take on—and

beat—some of the biggest names in world-class motor racing. And it all began with this car.

Over time, LXO126 was sold and ultimately acquired by noted British collector and enthusiast Dick Skipworth, who not only actively campaigned the car in classic events but was also able to reunite many of the original Ecurie Ecosse cars back under one roof.

After this cornerstone car and several of its brethren were auctioned by Bonhams in 2013, Jaguar Design Director Ian Callum and comedian Jay Leno drove it in the 2014 Mille Miglia, much to the delight of all.

Ecurie Ecosse would take on and beat some of the biggest names in world-class motor racing. And it all began with this car.

ECURIE ECOSSE JAGUAR
XK120 ROADSTER

| **Engine:** | 3442 cc, 6-cylinder | **Chassis no.:** | 660578 |
| **Horsepower:** | 160 | **Engine no.:** | W28687 |

Sole surviving Ecurie Ecosse founding car.
Third place winner in the Reims GP.

Sold at Bonhams December Sale, London, December 2013, for £707,100—a world record for the model.

1952

JAGUAR C-TYPE

In 1953, flush with a respectable measure of success from its first competitive year, Ecurie Ecosse replaced their fleet of Jaguar XK120s with Jaguar C-Types. The C-Type was the top of line for the Coventry, England-based marque and had already proven itself in its very first outing by winning the 1951 24 Hours of Le Mans outright.

While essentially sharing the same powertrain as its predecessor, the XK120, the C-Type's construction was radically different. Instead of a steel ladder frame with a pressed steel body like the XK120, the C-Type's frame was a lightweight tubular design covered by a simple but aerodynamic and lightweight aluminum body. Sporting newly developed disc brakes, triple twin-choke Weber carburetors, and high-lift camshafts, the car was nearly unbeatable in the right hands.

This C-Type, chassis number XKC042, was purchased new for the 1953 season and raced by Ecurie Ecosse drivers Ninian Sanderson to second place at Charterhall, Sir James Scott Douglas to third place at Ibsley, Jock Lawrence to second place at Snetterton and third place at Thurxton, and Jimmy Stewart to third place again at Charterhall.

At the Nürburgring 1000 km, against a field of over 50 entries, co-drivers Jimmy Stewart and Jock Lawrence took the car to an impressive sixth place and by doing so helped teammates Ian Stewart and Roy Salvadori take second place in their C-Type.

For the next season, Ecurie Ecosse owner David Murray sold the car to an amateur racer who campaigned it in Britain and France before selling it to Englishman David Elkan in 1960.

Elkan entered the C-Type in the odd hill climb but mostly enjoyed it simply as a fast road car. In anticipation of his wedding, Elkan affixed a full-length windshield

and luggage rack to the car and then sped off on his honeymoon with his new bride. Driving from London to Paris, across France down to Cannes, and then over to Barcelona before ferrying it to Mallorca, he recalled how the happy couple in their C-Type impressed everyone as they pulled up to The Ritz Hotel in Paris.

After 11 years in Mallorca where, in Elkan's words, he "did several hill climbs as it (the C-Type) was one of the most exciting cars on the island," the car returned to England and was sold.

Years later, in 1992, the former Ecurie Ecosse warriorr was bought by Dick Skipworth, subsequently forming

the core around which the magnificent Skipworth Ecurie Ecosse Collection evolved in the 2000s.

Skipworth and his son thoroughly enjoyed the car, having run it at the Monaco Historic Grand Prix, Goodwood Festival of Speed, Goodwood Revival, Mille Miglia Storica, Classica Italia, and Woodcote Trophy, among other events. Before consigning to it auction with Bonhams, Skipworth reminisced:

"She has been driven on many occasions by celebrities Stirling Moss, Tony Brooks, Jackie Stewart and Barrie 'Whizzo' Williams. I have come to regard her as the second lady in my life, always responsive, impeccably mannered,

exciting when provoked, gracious lines, totally reliable, not too expensive to maintain, well mannered in traffic but prefers the open road, and holds her own in younger company. I guess there is not much wrong."

The nose stripes signified rank so the pit crew could recognize which car was headed towards them. This was the team's sergeant.

ECURIE ECOSSE JAGUAR C-TYPE
SPORTS RACING ROADSTER

| Engine: | 3442 cc, 6-cylinder | Chassis no.: | XKC 042 |
| Horsepower: | 210 | Engine no.: | E1042-8 |

Achieved sixth place in the Nürburgring 1000 km.

Sold at Bonhams December Sale, London, December 2013, for £2,913,500—a world auction record for the model.

1956

JAGUAR D-TYPE

In 1956, the year in which this specific car—chassis number XKD561—was raced, the season was particularly busy with the Ecurie Ecosse team competing in no fewer than 20 races, winning six of them. Raced in 12 events that year in Great Britain, France, and Belgium, this car achieved splendid results from the following team drivers: Ron Flockhart won first and second in two races at Snetterton, first at Goodwood, second at Oulton Park, and third at Silverstone; Desmond Titterington clinched second at Aintree; and Peter Hughs got two second places in two races at Charterhall.

Ron Flockhart's exploits in the new car at Snetterton that Easter weekend in March were described as follows in *Autosport* magazine:

"George Abecassis made a beautiful start (in his HWM)...Flockhart (in his Jaguar) was after him like a greyhound chasing an electric hare. The Abecassis-Flockhart duel was one of drum brakes versus disc. The Jaguar closed up, and eventually, just halfway through the race, the disc brakes won. Flockhart took the lead and kept it, though not by very much. That it was Flockhart's day (his first for Ecurie Ecosse and first in a D-Type) was borne out by the last race, a 10-lap handicap for everyone. From ninth place on the first lap, the Scotsman climbed to third on the sixth lap, and second on the eighth, catching the leader at a pace of 3 seconds per lap."

At Aintree, Titterington was only bested in the car by Roy Salvadori driving the factory-entered Aston Martin DBS3, and at Silverstone by Salvadori in the Aston again and Stirling Moss in the factory-entered Maserati 300S—the highest caliber of competition to be sure. That a private team could go toe-to-toe with the biggest in the industry said volumes about the Ecurie Ecosse drivers and cars.

Like most good racing machines, the D-Type passed hands several times until it entered the fold of renowned

Just as the C-Type was built specifically to win the 24 Hours of Le Mans, so too was the D-Type created to win motor racing's most prestigious event.

Although it was powered by what was essentially the same albeit improved version of the C-Type's XK competition engine, the D-Type—like the C-Type succeeding the XK120 before it—varied from its predecessor significantly by way of structural design. Applying aeronautical technology to its cars, the D-Type's structure was of a new, revolutionary monocoque design to which two chassis "sub-frames" were bolted, giving the car great strength and significant weight reduction, not to mention more torsional stiffness.

In keeping with aeronautic principles, the aluminum alloy coachwork was a beautiful study of aerodynamics created by Malcolm Sayer, who had also designed the C-Type. The evocative elliptical shape reduced drag while the fin provided stability at high speeds.

The model was a masterpiece of design—for physics and aesthetics—and would soon (after some initial teething problems) prove its mettle again and again. Most notably, the D-Type won Le Mans an astounding three years in a row—the first in 1955 by the Jaguar factory team and then in 1956 and 1957 by Ecurie Ecosse, with the last year seeing total domination with first, second, third, fourth, *and* sixth places taken by D-Types!

British enthusiast and collector Dick Skipworth, under whose stewardship it ran a number of classic events including Goodwood Revival and Le Mans Classic.

With its innovative design and its dominating performance, the Jaguar D-Type is today regarded as one the greatest competition cars ever built. During its tenure it was one of the fastest (and most beautiful) cars on the track and in 1957 it was totally unassailable.

ECURIE ECOSSE JAGUAR D-TYPE
"SHORT NOSE" SPORTS RACING TWO-SEATER

Engine:	3442 cc, 6-cylinder	**Chassis no.:**	XKD 561
Horsepower:	250	**Engine no.:**	E2010-9

Raced in the Rouen GP, Silverstone GP, Belgian GP, and many more.

Sold at Bonhams December Sale, London, December 2013, for £2,577,500—a world auction record for the model.

1960

COMMER TS3

The Ecurie Ecosse team had relied upon a pair of converted coach transporters throughout the 1950s, but once David Murray's D-Type Jaguars had not only won their second consecutive 24 Hours of Le Mans in 1957 but had also come home first and second in the world's most prestigious endurance race, membership of their Ecurie Ecosse Association supporters club absolutely boomed.

Collectively, association members were eager to help the team's racing efforts. After all, Ecurie Ecosse had become the pride of Britain and national heroes of Scotland.

With their home base in Edinburgh, a proper, new transporter—one befitting champions—was needed and there were several prominent individuals willing to assist. Association member Alistair Cormack, managing director of James Ross & Sons, agents for Rootes Group, automotive manufacturers, and parent company to Commer commercial vehicles, came forward to help acquire a suitable vehicle, while Ronnie Alexander, managing director of Walter Alexander & Company, specialist truck and bus coachbuilders, offered to have a one-off transporter designed and built by his firm. Further support for the project was offered by British Aluminium (paneling), Dunlop, Lucas Industries, and Wilmot Breeden parts suppliers, among others, with machining and other services donated by companies such as John Gibson & Sons. And so work began on the team's brand-new transporter in 1959, made possible by the Ecurie Ecosse Association and its legion of supporters.

Walter Alexander's design manager, Selby Howgate, was a good-humored, colorful character within the Scottish motoring world. He had trained as an aerodynamicist in the British aviation industry and was a tremendous Bentley enthusiast, always seen driving his thunderous 4.5-liter model with vigor, usually while swathed in heavy tweeds. Howgate's assistant, Ian Johnston, would later recall that

had this Commer transporter for Ecurie Ecosse been an actual commercial project it would have cost an absolute fortune. This was because the ever-ebullient design manager kept changing his mind, but in the end created something that has been described as being "…nothing short of stunning in concept and execution." Many people have commented on the upward sweep at the rear of the bodywork, which Johnston explains was the answer to Selby's rhetorical question: "What is the most streamlined thing in nature…a fish."

The transporter emerged with a spacious cab for the Commer's crew plus a six-foot by six-foot square workshop area behind, providing a work bench and vice, which also gave car-underside access on the upper deck. One car could be accommodated on the bottom deck and two up top, while a single hydraulic ram located under the floor raised and lowered the upper ramp via cables.

The ingenious, bespoke Commer transporter was finished in time for the 1960 motor racing season and was used until the team's retirement in 1971. Wherever it traveled, the Ecurie Ecosse transporter always attracted a crowd.

Over time the Commer was sold to various owners and ultimately fell into disrepair, rendering it nearly useless. One day, decades later, Ecurie Ecosse enthusiast and collector Dick Skipworth—who by then owned a former Ecurie Ecosse Jaguar C-Type—acquired the team transporter and had it exhaustively restored by Jaguar specialists Lynx.

Skipworth's rescue and subsequent restoration gave the transporter new life and from the mid-2000s up until its sale by Bonhams in 2013 it could be seen ferrying a trio of Ecurie Ecosse cars to motoring events around Europe.

It has been written that, "The new Ecurie Ecosse vehicle was without doubt the most memorable of all the transporters from that era, eye-catching in the extreme, with its long, rakish lines and forward-sloping windscreen to allow the upper ramps to run the full length of the vehicle. Finished in the usual Ault & Wiborg Flag Metallic Blue with smart gold signwriting on either side, it turned heads wherever it went, its unique exhaust note giving advanced warning of its approach…"

It is interesting to note that as one of the most instantly recognizable team transporters ever, the Ecurie Ecosse Commer was created in 1:8 scale-model by the Corgi Toy brand after it made its debut. Today, over 50 years later, these models still hold such strong interest that examples in mint condition sell for hundreds of dollars.

The real 1:1 scale transporter used by the team, however, is totally inimitable. As a custom-built one-off, it has no equal and stands proudly alone in the spotlight of motoring history.

Wherever it traveled, the transporter always attracted a crowd.

ECURIE COMMER TS3
THREE-CAR TRANSPORTER

| **Engine:** | 3.2-liter, 3-cylinder | **Chassis no.:** | T99A2181 |
| **Horsepower:** | 105 | | |

Coachwork by Walter Alexander.

Sold at Bonhams December Sale, London, December 2013, for £1,793,500—a world auction record for the marque.

1954-1963
MERCEDES-BENZ *300 SL*
"GULLWING" COUPE & ROADSTER

Born from enormous racing success…
an undisputed icon of mid–century design…
it is no exaggeration to say that it
is one of the greatest cars ever made.

The 300 SL is an undisputed icon of mid-century design and a hallmark of one of the world's most important automobile manufacturers. Its sensual, evocative lines elicit emotion, regularly earning it the title of one of history's most beautiful cars, while its performance impresses even the harshest critic. It is no exaggeration to say that the 300 SL, particularly the coupe, is one of the greatest cars ever made. And it owes its existence to a salesman by the name of Max Hoffman.

To be clear, Mercedes-Benz designer Rudolf Uhlenhaut was responsible for the W194, the father of the 300 SL. It was developed purely as a race car for the 1952

Grand Prix season and was built around a highly advanced welded aluminum tube chassis, which greatly reduced weight without compromising strength. Because of this unique design, traditional doors were impossible to fit so rooftop doors were invented. It was an entirely practical solution to a unique challenge but quickly become regarded as a design innovation.

While the primary virtue of the streamlined, aluminum clad W194 was its light weight and low drag, it also benefitted from innovative design upgrades to the intelligently rearranged engine—namely an aluminum diagonal head that allowed for larger intake and exhaust valves—as well as relatively precise steering and four-wheel independent suspension. When put to the test, the W194 proved massively potent.

It boasted the very first production fuel-injection (increasing power to greater than that of the original racing version!) and the world's fastest top speed.

Despite being outpowered by rivals Ferrari and Jaguar, the Mercedes-Benz W194 proved that success lay in more than just raw horsepower. It was from this glorious pedigree that the 300 SL was born.

Straight out of the gate it won second and fourth places in the Mille Miglia, next a full podium sweep in the Bern GP, and then clinched first and second places at the 24 Hours of Le Mans. It was the first time a German car had won the world's most prestigious race. As if that were not enough, the W194 went on to win astonishing first, second, third, *and* fourth places in the Nürburgring GP and then took first and second in the Carrera Pan-Americana.

Max Hoffman was the Mercedes-Benz importer in the United States and, upon seeing the enormous racing success of the distinctive, eye-catching W194, suggested to company management that a road going version of the racer be made for the American market. The result was the 3-liter *Sport Leicht,* or 300 "Light Sport" abbreviated to SL.

The car was introduced at the 1954 New York Auto Show (instead of the typical Geneva or Frankfurt shows)

It was essentially a Grand Prix champion fitted with creature comforts. It was beautiful, exotic, modern, pedigreed, wholly unique, and brimming with excitement.

MERCEDES-BENZ 300 SL "GULLWING"

Engine:	2996 cc, 6-cylinder	**Chassis no.:**	198.040.4500130
Horsepower:	215	**Engine no.:**	198.980.4500145

Formerly owned by musician Pat Boone.

Sold at Bonhams Quail Lodge Auction, Carmel, August 2014, for $1,347,500.

1963

ROADSTER

with the aim of appealing directly to its intended audience: Americans. It was an instant success. The 300 SL Coupe caused a sensation among attendees and the media, who dubbed it the "gullwing" due to the open doors' resemblance of outspread wings.

Here was an avant-garde road car that was essentially a Grand Prix champion fitted with creature comforts. It was beautiful, exotic, modern, pedigreed, wholly unique, and brimming with excitement. Furthermore, it was pleasurable to drive. This Teutonic marvel boasted the very

first production fuel-injection (increasing power to greater than that of the original racing version) and the world's fastest top speed. Orders poured in despite the high cost, and in one fell swoop Mercedes-Benz transformed its hitherto image in America of somber luxury sedan manufacturer into that of a high-performance sports car maker.

After selling some 1400 Gullwings—the vast majority to Americans—Mercedes-Benz introduced a convertible successor. In 1957, the 300 SL Roadster debuted with its removable hard top and retractable soft top, and although

it was more expensive than the Coupe it was nonetheless a great success with over 1850 cars ultimately being made.

Based on the same chassis as the Coupe, the Roadster incorporated a strengthened tube frame chassis to maintain rigidity and strength. Additional improvements included revising the rear suspension for better stability during high-speed cornering and later adding four-wheel disc brakes and an all-alloy engine toward the end of the model's production run.

Both the Coupe and Roadster models were a marvel of engineering and design, and with a top speed of 150 mph (a truly astounding velocity for the day) these refined luxury sports cars never strayed from their racing roots. Furthermore, unlike many exclusive automobiles, the 300 SL was commercially successful. Add to that the change of perception it initiated in the world's largest consumer market, and it can be argued that the 300 SL forever altered the fortunes of Mercedes-Benz.

Today, both versions of the 300 SL are considered some of the most sought after collector's cars of all time and eternally regarded as icons of the automotive industry.

MERCEDES-BENZ 300 SL ROADSTER

Engine:	2996 cc, 6-cylinder	**Chassis no.:**	198042.10.003174
Horsepower:	225	**Engine no.:**	198982.10.000137

Desirable alloy engine block and disc brakes.

Sold at Bonhams Quail Lodge Auction, Carmel, August 2014, for $1,815,000.

1954
MERCEDES-BENZ
W196R F1
FORMULA 1 FACTORY
RACING SINGLE-SEATER

*The symbolic reemergence of Germany
as a world (motorsport) power had begun.*

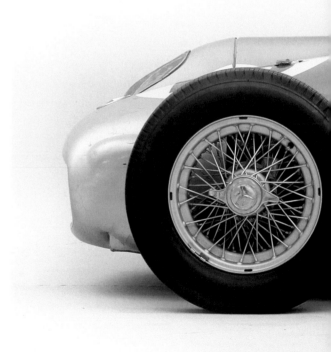

The unbeatable combination of Germany's W196R silver arrow and Argentina's driving maestro Juan Manuel Fangio is a story of greatness, and one that would not exist without the other.

This incredible story began in the years immediately following the Second World War, when German industry was emerging from the cataclysm of that obliterating war. Automotive historian Karl Ludvigsen described how, in the late 1940s, if anyone enquired about a possible return to racing they would be told, "Please, we are fighting for our very lives. We have no time to think of such things."

In a move never before seen in the history of the world, the United States provided a "life line" to war-ravaged western European nations—allies and former enemies alike. The European Recovery Program of 1948, better known as the Marshall Plan, pumped $17-billion into these devastated economies. Germany received a sizeable share and Daimler-Benz, which was making bicycles and

servicing the Jeeps of the occupying US forces—anything to stay alive—was able to ramp up production enabling Mercedes-Benz to once again think about racing.

Emblematic of the industriousness of the German people, the emergence of Mercedes-Benz from the ashes of total war in such a short time was truly astonishing.

Just fours years later in 1952, Mercedes-Benz introduced the W194 (the father of the iconic 300 SL), which vaulted to the top of world competition. Then, in 1954, the Stuttgart-based company unveiled its next world-beater: the W196.

Motor Sport magazine set the scene when it wrote: "The name of Mercedes-Benz was one of the most powerful in Grand Prix racing between 1934 and 1939, and during those years they brought a science into motor racing that was revolutionary; at the same time they speeded up the process of racing car design to a pace that forced many of their competitors to abandon Grand Prix racing...With the approach of the new Formula 1 that was due to begin with

The emergence of Mercedes-Benz from the ashes of total war ... to the top of world competition ... in such a short time was truly astonishing.

the 1954 season, Daimler-Benz announced that they would be represented ... by an *entirely new* team of Mercedes-Benz racing cars."

When these new streamline-bodied W196 cars emerged for the first time at Reims, people recoiled in astonishment. These sleek new silver arrows, as they were called (more appropriate would be rocket ships), with their wheel-enclosing body shells were futuristically alien machines. Drivers Fangio and Karl Kling immediately qualified first and second and then promptly finished first and second in their debut race—more than a lap ahead of the third-placed Ferrari. The public and media were aghast.

These new cars were the result of the development of an all-new 2.5-liter, non-supercharged, roller-bearing engine. Breaking new ground, they successfully introduced to Formula 1 the lightweight spaceframe or tube chassis construction (similar to that used on the W125 and W194), fuel-injected, straight-eight "laydown" engines

with desmodromic valve actuation, all-round, inboard-mounted brakes, and all-independent suspension with low-pivot swing-axles at the rear. These supremely complex cars, the product of chief designer Rudolf Uhlenhaut, were pure mechanical genius. The result was both physical and psychological, and in just one weekend Formula 1 had progressed nearly a quarter century. The symbolic reemergence of Germany as a world power had begun.

These supremely complex cars were pure mechanical genius. In just one weekend F1 had progressed nearly a quarter century.

Although the W196 streamliner bodies were unbeatable on circuits with fast straights and slow corners, they were vulnerable on twisty tracks as the enclosed wheels prevented the pilots from precise wheel placement. To rectify this, Uhlenhaut's team constructed an open-wheel *monoposto* body that Fangio took all the way to the checkered flag. And this is the very car in which he did it.

Winning the German GP at Nürburgring and then the Swiss GP at Bremgarten—both at more than a minute

ahead of second place—the gifted Fangio was able to clinch what would be the second of his five World Championship titles.

Widely acknowledged as one of the world's greatest drivers, if not the best, Fangio's records are still unbeaten today with the highest winning percentage of any F1 driver, highest percentage of pole positions, highest percentage of front row starts, and the oldest World Champion in the sport.

As a championship car driven by a championship pilot at a critical, formative time in German *and* world history, this W196R is not just a milestone but also an automotive, cultural, and historical heritage.

MERCEDES-BENZ W196R FORMULA 1
FACTORY RACING SINGLE-SEATER

Engine:	2496 cc, 8-cylinder	**Chassis no.:**	196 010 00006/54
Horse Power:	290	**Engine no.:**	0006/54

Driven by Manuel Fangio to his second World Championship title. Winner of the Swiss GP and German GP. Only surviving W196R to have won two World Championship-qualifying GPs

Sold at Bonhams Goodwood Festival of Speed Sale, Chichester, July 2013, for £19,601,500—a world auction record for any car sold at auction.

1955
MASERATI *300S*
SPORTS-RACING SPIDER

"It is one of my favorite…Maseratis…
one of the easiest, nicest, best-balanced
sports-racing cars ever made."

- Stirling Moss

R acing great Stirling Moss, who won both the 1956 Buenos Aires 1000 km and Nürburgring 1000 km in a Maserati 300S, said of this car: *"It is one of my favorite front-engined sports Maseratis…one of the easiest, nicest, best-balanced sports-racing cars ever made."*

Built specifically to compete against the larger capacity cars from Ferrari and Jaguar, Maserati engineers developed their successful 250F engine into what would become the beefy, all-aluminum, straight six-cylinder 300S engine. Featuring a twin overhead camshaft cylinder head with three 45 mm Weber carburetors, the effectively 3000 cc 300S was capable of producing 260 bhp and battling quite effectively against its rivals.

The chassis was a modern, intricate spaceframe design, which, like all tubular-style frames, greatly reduced weight without sacrificing rigidity and strength. The process was extremely labor intensive and expensive but far superior to conventional chassis, and by this time nearly all the major factories engaged in racing were employing this method.

The aluminum paneled body, created by Fantuzzi coachbuilders, was likewise light in weight, aerodynamic, and boasted beautiful proportions. Although purpose-built to win races, the car—in typical Italian style—appears predatory yet sensual; a contradictory but somehow complimentary realization.

This particular 300S, chassis number 3053, was ordered new from Modena by famous American sportsman Briggs Cunningham. A successful racing car driver, builder,

team owner, and collector, Cunningham was also an accomplished sailor who, as skipper, won the prestigious America's Cup and earned himself a place in both the America's Cup Hall of Fame and Motorsports Hall of Fame.

Purpose-built to win races, it appears predatory yet sensual; a contradictory but somehow complimentary realization.

Upon delivery of the car, Cunningham's friend and team driver Bill Spear raced it in a number of races during the 1955 season, including the 12 Hours of Sebring where it placed third and the United States GP at Watkins Glen where it placed second. Sold after a full roster of American races, the 300S continued to be campaigned in amateur events by subsequent owners.

While competitive and successful, not to mention extremely attractive, the beauty of Maserati's 300S lies in the fact that it is also very versatile and not a car relegated to the track. This virtue, combined with all the many others, makes this car highly desirable a true road and track automobile.

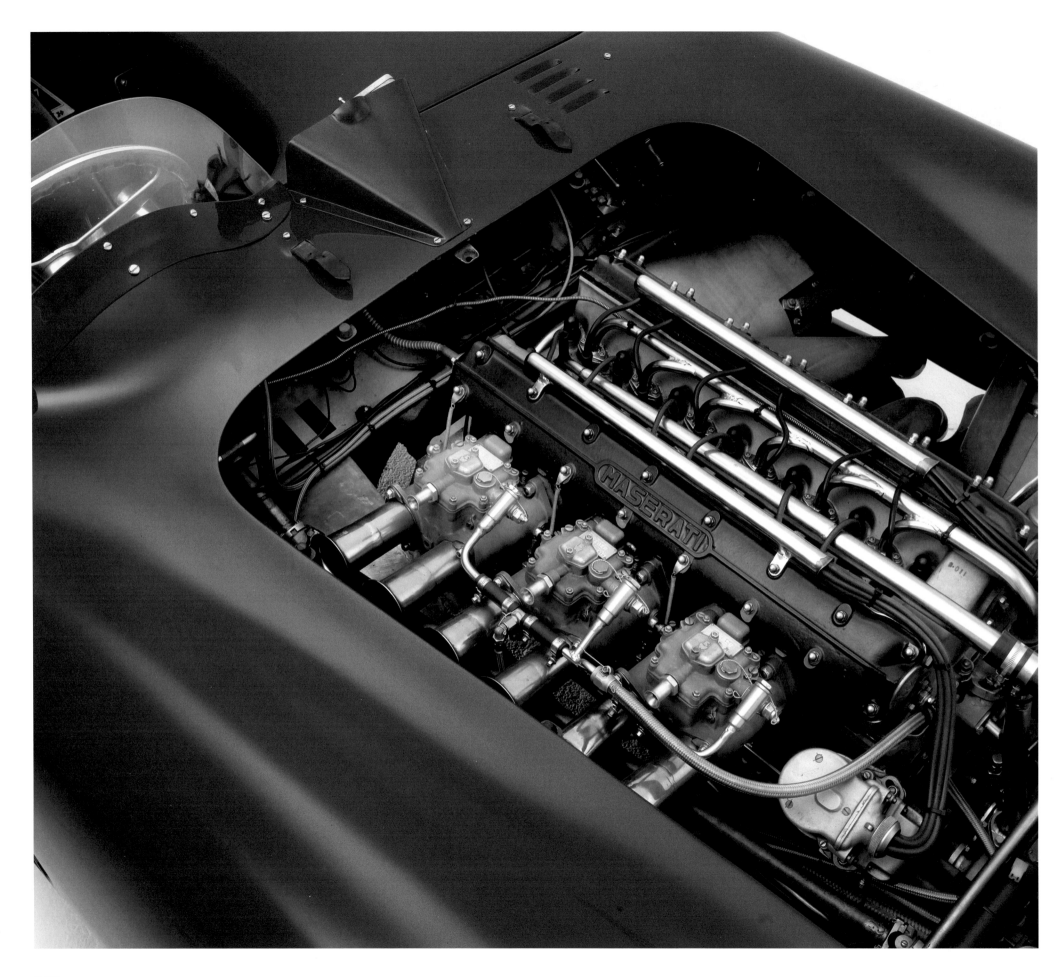

MASERATI 300S
SPORTS-RACING SPIDER

Coachwork by Fantuzzi. Ordered new by Briggs Cunningham.
Raced in the 12 Hours of Sebring, United States GP, and more.

Engine:	2991 cc, 6-cylinder	**Chassis no.:**	3053
Horsepower:	260	**Engine no.:**	3053

Sold at Bonhams Goodwood Festival of Speed Sale, Chichester, July 2013, for £4,033,500—a world auction record for the marque.

1957
PORSCHE *356A*
1600 SPEEDSTER

"A product that is coherent in form requires no embellishment. It is enhanced by the purity of its form."

– F.A. "Bützi" Porsche

The Porsche 356 was the first production car built by the eponymous firm, first in a converted saw-mill in Gmünd, Austria, before relocating shortly thereafter to Stuttgart, Germany. Ferdinand "Ferry" Porsche, son of company founder Dr. Ferdinand Porsche, designed the 356 with the following rationale:

"I saw that if you had enough power in a small car it is nicer to drive than if you have a big car which is over-powered. And it is more fun. On this basic idea we start-ed the first Porsche prototype. To make the car lighter, to have an engine with more horsepower...that was the first two-seater that we built."

Successful in racing from the day it debuted, the new Porsche sports car soon became renowned—mostly in the Germanic countries—for its sprightliness, superb handling, and excellent build quality. By the time Americans started to take notice of Porsche, the roads in the US were filled with lightweight, fast, and inexpensive British sports cars.

In the early 1950s, a Porsche coupe cost more than a Jaguar XK120, let alone an MG, Triumph, or Austin-Healey. So while the attributes of Porsche were admired, the car was simply too expensive by American standards, and this was negatively affecting growth in the world's largest market.

Max Hoffman, the Porsche importer in the United States (and the man that convinced Mercedes-Benz to create the enormously successful 300 SL "Gullwing" for the American market), recognized the need for a sportier, less expensive German car to compete with the popular British imports and made the recommendation to Porsche.

The engineers in Stuttgart immediately set to work creating a less expensive yet nonetheless sporty example by essentially offering a car devoid of trimmings, weather protection, and creature comforts—all of which led to not just cost savings but also weight savings. The new model, dubbed the Speedster, had a smaller, low-profile, retractable top, a low, raked windscreen that could easily be removed for racing, lightweight bucket seats with fixed backrests, window curtains instead of roll-up windows, and instrumentation that consisted of only a speedometer and temperature gauge. Even a heater was optional. On the performance side, the weight savings increased the speed of the car handsomely and the engine, first offered in 1500 cc, was later increased to 1600 cc.

This "economy" version of Porsche's 356 Cabriolet was an instant hit, especially in southern California, where weather was rarely a concern and the amateur racing scene was flourishing. Even the press were impressed, with *Road & Track*—apparently unaffected by the spartan interior—saying: "A more comfortable sports car for long, high-speed journeys would be very hard to find, and certainly no other car achieves the combination of comfort, performance, and fuel economy of the Porsche."

With great styling, superb handling, and excellent value-for-money, the Porsche Speedster was the perfect recipe. Not only that, but it was sexy and could win races. Owned and raced by the likes of James Dean (prior to his acquisition of the Spyder) and Steve McQueen, the Porsche Speedster quickly gained an image of the exciting, fast, and carefree California lifestyle. Today, far from its bargain roots, the Speedster is a highly coveted collector car that far exceeds the value of its other 356-variant brethren.

PORSCHE 356A
1600 SPEEDSTER

Engine:	1582 cc, 4-cylinder	Chassis no.:	84142
Horsepower:	90	Engine no.:	67751

Coachwork by Reutter.

Sold at Bonhams Scottsdale Auction, Scottsdale, January 2014, for $253,000.

1958
LISTER-CHEVROLET
"KNOBBLY" SPORTS-RACING TWO-SEATER

The Lister-Chevrolet and its Lister-Jaguar sibling were more than a match on the track for the dominant Ferrari and Jaguar cars of the day.

In 1958, the Lister-Jaguar was unveiled to the British motoring press at Cambridge. Its unique, muscle-bound body, although very curvaceous, was deemed "knobbly" by the media—a nickname it has lovingly carried to this day.

Brian Lister had styled this entirely distinctive body form to weave its way brilliantly through FIA Appendix C screen-height regulations and to minimize frontal area, despite the considerable height of the model's primary power unit—the iron-block, twin-overhead camshaft 6-cylinder Jaguar XK engine. The new design's nose section featured deeply scalloped valleys between the front wheel fenders and a central hump enclosing the engine that rose higher than the base of the windscreen. Flaring rear wings

enclosing the wheels and a shapely headrest behind the driver rounded out the design, which was athletic and forceful in appearance. To motor sportsmen of the day, the result was pure form following function, and the car took the world by storm.

To cover the lightweight, aerodynamic chassis, aluminum body panels were formed by Williams & Pritchard of north London. Len Pritchard had wartime aircraft industry experience of forming magnesium-alloy panels and suggested to Lister that panels in magnesium instead of aluminum could save half the weight, despite doubling the price. As a result, Lister was able to offer Knobbly bodies in aluminum or magnesium-alloy to customer choice.

Another option available to customers, primarily those on the western side of the Atlantic, was a small-block Chevrolet V8 engine. One of the most enthusiastic proponents of this combination was Carroll Shelby, and

one of the most visible Briggs Cunningham. The Lister-Chevrolet and its Lister-Jaguar sibling were more than a match on the track for the dominant Ferrari and Jaguar cars of the day.

This particular Lister-Chevrolet, chassis number BHL115, is exemplary because of its untouched condition. Completely original, which is quite rare for any race car, this Lister-Chevy was bought new and was then rarely if ever used. In 1992, more than three decades from when it was first built, the car participated in the Lister reunion at Lime Rock. In attendance was company founder Brian Lister who expressed amazement at "...absolutely the most amazing time-warp car I have ever seen." He found it doubly amazing that he could recognize much of the

typical, signature handiwork of his small team of British craftsman who handcrafted each car.

Down to its original Dunlop racing tires and Lucas "Le Mans 24" headlamp lenses, this well preserved "time machine" is an impressive artifact of motorsport history.

LISTER-CHEVROLET "KNOBBLY"
SPORTS-RACING TWO-SEATER

Engine:	4640 cc, 6-cylinder	**Chassis no.:**	BHL115
Horse Power:	300	**Engine no.:**	3731548

Coachwork by Williams & Pritchard. Completely original, unrestored example.

Sold at Bonhams Quail Lodge Sale, Carmel, August 2013, for $1,430,000.

1960
–
1969

1960
ASTON MARTIN *DB4 GT*
JET COUPE

The Aston Martin DB4 GT had emphatically demonstrated that a British manufacturer could better the Italians at their own game when it came to constructing the ultimate GT.

Coachbuilt examples of David Brown-era Aston Martins are extremely rare, making this unique Bertone-bodied car all the more precious. This car was the last DB4 GT chassis completed in this period (six Sanction II/III DB4 GT Zagatos were built in the late 1980s and early 1990s) and was first displayed on Carrozzeria Bertone's stand at the 1961 Geneva Motor Show. Its designer was none other than Giorgetto Giugiaro, one of the twentieth century's century's foremost automotive stylists, then only 22 years of age, who would go on to create some of Italy's most memorable designs under Bertone and Ghia. By the time he ventured on his own to found Italdesign in 1968,

Giugiaro had been responsible for such creations as the Maserati Ghibli and De Tomaso Mangusta.

It was only appropriate that Aston Martin's top-of-the range and most expensive production model, the DB4 GT, should have been selected for this very special project. As its nomenclature suggests, this David Brown fourth series model was, as a Grand Tourer, a competition variant of the DB4 sports saloon. Launched at the London Motor Show in 1959, the Aston Martin DB4 GT had emphatically demonstrated that a British manufacturer could better the Italians (read Ferrari) at their own game when it came to constructing the ultimate GT. Its specification included a new steel platform chassis with disc brakes and a race-developed, twin-camshaft, six-cylinder 3.7-liter engine, all clothed in a perfectly proportioned aluminum body designed by Carrozzeria Touring of Milan. Overall, the DB4

GT was state-of-the-art for its time, a masterstroke of British engineering combined with exquisite Italian styling.

The the DB4's immensely strong platform-type chassis replaced a multi-tubular spaceframe, the latter being considered incompatible with Touring's Superleggera body construction that employed its own lightweight tubular structure to support the hand-formed aluminum-body panels.

The new car's competition potential had been recognized from the outset and the factory lost no time in developing a lightweight version suitable for racing. In 1959, before the debut at the London Motor Show, Stirling Moss drove the GT prototype to its first win at Silverstone. Extensive modifications to the standard car took five inches (12.7 cm) out of the wheelbase and replaced the rear seats with a luggage platform on all but a small num-

"It was meant to be a grand tourer and that's just what I used it for."

ber of cars. Together with lighter, 18-gauge bodywork by Touring, these changes reduced the car's weight by around 200 lbs (91 kg).

The DB4 GT used a tuned engine that, equipped with a twin-plug cylinder head and triple Weber 45DCOE carburetors, produced 302 bhp at 6,000 rpm, a useful increase over the standard car's 240 bhp. Maximum speed, of course, depended on overall gearing, but 153 mph was achieved during testing with a 0-60 mph time of 6.1 seconds recorded. The DB4 GT was also one of the first cars

The DB4 GT was state-of-the-art for its time, a masterstroke of British engineering combined with exquisite Italian styling.

to go from standstill to 100 mph and then brake to a dead stop in under 20 seconds, a tribute, in part, to its uprated Girling brakes. The result was a true dual-purpose car, equally at ease on both the road and the track.

Approximately 75 DB4 GTs were produced, with just 30 in left-hand drive configuration. Another 19 were bodied by Zagato and only one—this one—was bodied by Bertone.

The "Jet," as it became known, was even more unique in that it was the only DB4 GT example to be bodied in steel—an attribute that, according to Bertone, would have made much more of an impact (and resulted in more sales) had its Geneva debut not coincided with that of the Jaguar E-Type, a vehicle consistently named the sexiest car in the world.

Eventually sold to a private buyer, the sole existing Bertone DB4 GT spent time in Lebanon and later the United States before being discovered in very poor condition by Aston Martin's chairman in the 1980s. Shipped back to England for a thorough and accurate restoration by the Aston Martin factory in Newport Pagnell, the car would prove very challenging to restore due to its bespoke Italian nature. Nevertheless, with patience and perseverance

the Jet was brought back to its original glory and sold to a Swiss enthusiast who used it as its maker intended. He declared, "It was meant to be a grand tourer and that's just what I used it for," including one marathon trip from San Francisco to Vancouver—a distance of 950 miles (1530 km)—in one day!

In addition to being an excellent performer, the car was also greatly admired and went on to win numerous awards at prestigious shows such as the Pebble Beach Concours d'Elegance and the Concorso d'Eleganza Villa d' Este—a testament to its excellent restoration, historical value, rarity, and superb qualities as an elite sports car.

ASTON MARTIN DB4 GT
JET COUPE

Engine:	3.7-liter, 6-cylinder	**Chassis no.:**	0201L
Horsepower:	300	**Engine no.:**	370/0201/GT

Coachwork by Bertone. Sole example built.

Sold at Bonhams Aston Martin Works Sale, Newport Pagnell, May 2013 for £3,249,500—a world auction record for the marque.

1960
JAGUAR *E2A*
RACING TWO-SEATER FACTORY PROTOTYPE "MISSING LINK"

As the taproot of the glorious E–Type and with its racing history and rarity, it is simply a monumental car.

This one-off Jaguar prototype, known by its chassis number E2A, is one of the most significant prototypes ever produced by the mainstream motor industry. Known as the "missing link" due to it succeeding the legendary D-Type and preceding the everlasting E-Type, this evolutionary masterpiece—one that was never given a formal model name—was driven by four of the world's greatest racing drivers and then remained unmolested in single family ownership for over four decades. Such a car is the stuff of dreams and this is how it began.

By 1960, a Jaguar had won the world's most prestigious motor race, the 24 Hours of Le Mans, no fewer than five times, twice with a C-Type and three times with a D-Type. The Jaguar company had withdrawn from factory-sponsored competition after 1956, but had con-

tinued to maintain a racing presence through customer teams such as Briggs Cunningham in America and Ecurie Ecosse in Scotland.

Building upon its racing pedigree, Jaguar was to produce an all-new semi-monocoque chassis design that was to emerge in 1961 as the E-Type. The prototype for this model would be effected through an order placed by Cunningham in anticipation for Le Mans, and the result was the E2A, or what many at the time called the "Cunningham E-Type." As the next evolutionary step for Jaguar, it was meant by the Coventry-based company to test several features of the forthcoming E-Type production model, not least its independent rear suspension system in place of the live-axle featured in D-Type design.

Completed in February 1960, the car was powered by an aluminum block, fuel-injected, 3-liter engine and finished for the Cunningham team in their famous American racing colors of white with two blue centerline stripes. Visually,

the car's tail-finned rear bodywork recalled the charismatic D-Type, while its handsomely proportioned one-piece forward bodywork presaged the lovely lines of the forthcoming E-Type.

At the 24 Hours of Le Mans that June, Cunningham entrusted the car to Dan Gurney and Walt Hansgen. They ran the car successfully well into the night but fuel-injection pipe failures created a weak mixture that caused burned pistons and a blown cylinder head gasket. The car was forced into retirement after completing 89 laps. It should be noted, however, that in the April tests prior to the race, Hansgen set the second fastest overall lap time at Le Mans, averaging 125 mph and splitting the Ferrari factory team's latest V12-engined 250 Testa Rossa Indipendente. On the Mulsanne straight, the E2A reached an incredible speed of 194.29 mph. Power and aerodynamics were certainly bred into Jaguar's new car.

For its American racing debut in August of 1960 at Bridgehampton, New York, Hansgen led throughout and won handsomely, beating such phenoms as the Maserati Tipo 61 "Birdcage." Two weeks later at Elkhart Lake, Wisconsin, Hansgen finished third and demonstrated not only his own skill in wet weather driving but also the capabilities of Jaguar's new, all-independent suspension.

In October 1960, the car ran the Grand Prix at Riverside, California, driven by Formula 1's new double-World Champion Jack Brabham, where it finished a distant tenth

On the Mulsanne Straight, it reached an incredible speed of 194.29 mph. Power and aerodynamics were certainly bred into Jaguar's new car.

place against much lighterweight free-Formula cars. And finally, for the Grand Prix at Laguna Seca, California, it was raced by Bruce McLaren before being sidelined by mechanical problems.

E2A then returned to England, where it was used by the factory for a number of purposes, including acting as a press decoy for the XJ13 V12 prototype and testing Dunlop's new Maxaret anti-lock braking system—the first ABS to be widely used and, interestingly, on mostly aircraft.

Ultimately, in the late 1960s Jaguar engineer Roger Woodley was successful in negotiating the purchase of E2A for his father-in-law, the prominent collector and racing photographer Guy Griffiths. It has remained unaltered in the Griffiths family up until Bonhams represented the car at auction in 2008.

All things considered, as the taproot of the glorious Jaguar E-Type series, prototype E2A would be enormously significant for that alone. But when one contemplates its racing history, its association with four all-time great racing drivers, its distinctiveness and rarity as a Jaguar model, and its original, factory-built condition, E2A offers just about the finest attributes anyone could ever seek in a road-useable sports-racing classic. It is simply a monumental car.

JAGUAR E2A LE MANS SPORTS-RACING TWO-SEATER FACTORY PROTOTYPE

Engine:	3-liter, 6-cylinder	**Chassis no.:**	E2A
Horsepower:	295	**Engine no.:**	E5028-10

Famous evolutionary "Missing Link" between D-Type and E-Type. Ordered by Briggs Cunningham for the 24 Hours of Le Mans. Driven by Dan Gurney, Walt Hansgen, Jack Brabham, and Bruce McLaren.

Sold at Bonhams Quail Lodge Auction, Carmel, August 2008, for $4,957,000—a world record for the marque.

1961
ASTON
MARTIN *DB4 GT*

An exclusive grand tourer boasting exquisite looks with impressive power and handling … the DB4 GT was an instant benchmark.

Created to best the Italians at their own game, which was building an exclusive grand tourer boasting exquisite looks with impressive power and handling, the Aston Martin DB4 GT was an instant benchmark. While this quintessential British sports racing car did feature Italian styling, the combination was tremendously complimentary and made the DB4 GT the pinnacle of mid-century English automotive.

Introduced in 1959, a year after the standard DB4 debuted, the GT was an immediate sensation. Both iterations of the David Brown fourth series car were initially bodied by Carrozzeria Touring of Milan, and such was the appeal that Aston Martin went on to commission two other Italian coachbuilding firms to apply their hand to the GT—Bertone and, most famously, Zagato. In all, some 95 DB4 GTs were manufactured between 1959 and 1963—75 bodied by

Touring, 19 by Zagato and 1 by Bertone. With less than 100 original variants made, demand has always exceeded supply, and today the value of DB4 GTs climbs ever higher.

With sports racing in mind, the GT was a highly uprated version of the already imposing DB4 and was made to be shorter, lighter, and faster. The aluminum-alloy, dual overhead-camshaft, 3.7-liter, six-cylinder engine with triple Weber carburetors delivered 302 bhp and speeds over 150 mph, while braking power was provided by four wheel Girling disc brakes attached to lightweight Borrani wire wheels. Inside, the seats were trimmed in sumptuous Connolly leather and the floors laid with Wilton wool carpet, while the *Superleggera* tubular body was wrapped in aluminum panels by Touring. The DB4 GT was a brute cloaked in a suit—muscle with style, rakish and refined, an exercise in powerful yet tastefully restrained sex appeal.

As Britain's fastest production car, the DB4 GT offered a strong challenge to prevailing Ferrari dominance and

179

It was a brute cloaked in a suit—muscle with style, rakish and refined, an exercise in powerful yet tastefully restrained sex appeal.

enjoyed several successes. One memorable triumph was at the Bahamas Speed Week of 1959, when the factory-entered DBR2 was rolled during practice. Without any backup, the team quickly borrowed a DB4 GT that had just been delivered to a Caribbean customer, which Stirling Moss promptly drove to victory.

Straight off the street to clinch the win, Aston Martin could not have dreamed of a better scenario.

This particular GT is one of just 30 produced in left-hand drive, making it even more unique among its uncommon brethren. A thoroughbred in every sense of the word, the Aston Martin DB4 GT is a highly useable, dual-purpose sports racer that represents a very special period of British motoring history.

ASTON MARTIN DB4 GT

Engine:	3.7-liter, 6-cylinder	Chassis no.:	0142L
Horsepower:	302	Engine no.:	370/0143/GT

Coachwork by Touring.

Sold at Bonhams Paris Sale, February 2012, for €1,012,000—a world auction record for the model.

1961

JAGUAR *E-TYPE*

SERIES I 3.8-LITER ROADSTER

No other automobile at the time took the world by such storm. Even Enzo Ferrari conceded that it was "the most beautiful car ever made."

Jaguar seemed to make a habit of shocking the automotive world. Sometimes the impact of its cars reached beyond the showrooms and exposition halls to rock popular culture, yet not even Jaguar's founder, Sir William Lyons, could have predicted the impact of the Jaguar E-Type. When introduced at the 1961 Geneva Motor Show, the new Jaguar stirred passions with its extremely sleek, curvaceous, forward thinking yet timeless design, backed up by staggering performance.

Constructed using methods derived from the D-Type sports racing car, the E-Type was a technical marvel. The light and rigid monocoque chassis used the engine itself as a structural part of the car, with the long and sleek bonnet, or hood, hinged at the front. The headlights were beautifully recessed in the fenders and enclosed with contoured Perspex coverings for a free flowing design

and improved aerodynamics. The car featured four-wheel independent suspension, disc brakes, and a Moss-type four-speed manual transmission. The proven XK power plant was carried over from the XK150 and made sure the lithe Jaguar would exceed the 150 mph mark—a truly incredible speed for a road car of its day.

Owned by the likes of George Harrison, Brigitte Bardot, Tony Curtis, Charlton Heston, Roy Orbison, and many other celebrities, the E-Type was, upon its debut, simply the "it" car. No other automobile at the time took the world by such storm. Even Enzo Ferrari famously conceded that it was "the most beautiful car ever made."

Three series of the E-Type were created during its standard production run from 1961 to 1975, with the first, Series I, being considered the most desirable and the convertible Roadster the most enviable of them all.

This particular E-Type was the 91st car built and as an early, first year example has the external bonnet latches preferred by collectors. As a left-hand drive model, it was

*Frequently called the most
beautiful car of all time,
it remains an icon of design,
engineering and speed.*

sold directly to the United States where it went on to be campaigned in hill climbs on the weekends to great success by future Austin-Healey factory team driver Jim Ladd.

Frequently called the most beautiful production car of all time, even a half century after its creation—a testament to its designer Malcolm Sayer—the E-Type remains an automotive icon of design, engineering, and speed.

JAGUAR E-TYPE SERIES I 3.8-LITER ROADSTER

Engine:	3.8-liter, 6-cylinder	**Chassis no.:**	875091
Horsepower:	265	**Engine no.:**	R1073-9

1 of first 100 built, 1 of 300 with external bonnet lock.

Sold at Bonhams Greenwich Concours d'Elegance Auction, Greenwich, June 2014, for $335,500.

1962
FERRARI *250 GT*
SHORT-WHEELBASE SPECIALE
AERODINAMICA

"This marvelous two-place coupe can certainly be considered as one of the most significant examples of the art of coach building…"

– Antoine Prunet

During the late 1950s through the 1960s, the successful Ferrari 250 Gran Turismo family of designs, with their front-mounted, 3-liter, V12 engines, provided the company with a firm foundation to expand its manufacturing volume. The 250 line from the Maranello-based firm was everything one could reasonably want in a GT—fast, strong and striking—and they were popular among affluent cognoscenti.

For those who wanted further exclusivity, there was the 400 Superamerica series of 4-liter, V12-engined models, the first of which was reputedly made for FIAT chief and style icon Gianni Agnelli. These were limited production cars offered to satisfy what was described as "the fastidiousness of a few perfectionists who demanded even more performance, comfort, and refinement, and who wanted even more of an image of prestige and exclusivity than could be provided by the 'standard' Ferrari."

At the 1960 Turin Auto Show, Ferrari and Pininfarina absolutely stunned the automotive world when they debuted the newest model in this elite category, the breathtaking Superfast II. It was an entirely new body shape for a performance car and incorporated painstaking detail throughout. In effect, it was an aerodynamically sleek GT limousine. Ferrari authority Antoine Prunet described the Superfast II as follows:

"This experimental creation by the great Torinese coachbuilder was actually quite remarkable for the completely new style which it proposed. Born in a wind tunnel, this harmonious design resembled the profile of an airplane wing. The leading edge was, in fact, the nose of the car, in the middle of which was the air intake for the radiator, an ellipse of very reduced dimensions resembling that of several

sports Ferraris. The trailing edge was represented by the rear deck, streamlined to a point upon which converged the curves of the roof. The graceful curve of the hood, devoid of all harshness, was particularly remarkable, as was the shape of the windshield, whose posts, very noticeably curved inward, reinforced the effect...This marvelous two-place coupe can certainly be considered as one of the most significant examples of the art of coachbuilding..."

Then came the Speciale Aerodinamica, which was essentially a bespoke blend of the 250 and 400. Individually commissioned by clients, they were custom-made specials

"Assembled like a bespoke suit, this is truly a unique vehicle."

– Fabrizio Violati

built on the short-wheelbase (SWB) chassis of the 250 GT but with 400 Superamerica-style bodywork. The benefit was the performance of the 250 with the luxury of the 400, not to mention the added exclusivity of singularity.

It is believed that only four of these Speciale Aerodinamica coupes were ever created, and it is from this very style that the GTO prototype car evolved to compete in the 1961 24 Hours of Le Mans, leading, ultimately, to the revered and most legendary Ferrari of them all—the 250 GTO.

Renowned Ferrari collector and owner of the this specific Speciale Aerodinamica, Fabrizio Violati, recalled:

"Enzo Ferrari used to welcome top politicians, sports heroes, and entertainers to his kingdom at Maranello when they came to pick up their (new car) directly from the hand of its creator. Chassis number 3615 was assembled like a bespoke suit, and this was the one and only time that this color appeared on a Ferrari. This is a truly unique vehicle, an amalgam of a 250 GT SWB chassis and engine in a body specially designed by Pininfarina and inspired by the Superamerica model..."

While these specially tailored machines never raced, they were certainly very capable cars and true to their Prancing Horse badges. In 1963 *Road & Track* tested a related 400 Superamerica and recorded a top speed of 179.6 mph (289 kph). The test car weighed a hefty 3710 lbs (1683 kg), so while this 250 GT SWB variant is considerably lighter and carries the more nimble 3-liter motor, its

performance would be quite comparable. Not only does this car combine its gloriously sleek Aerodinamica looks with deluxe accommodation and style, but it is also capable—for what is effectively a two-seater limousine—of quite prodigious performance.

Exclusive, rare, luxurious, and fast, this is the epitome of the caliber of work produced by the great collaborative talents of Ferrari and Pininfarina.

FERRARI 250 GT SHORT-WHEELBASE SPECIALE AERODINAMICA

Engine:	2953 cc, 12-cylinder	**Chassis no.:**	3615
Horsepower:	270	**Engine no.:**	314/62E

Coachwork by Pininfarina. 1 of 4 Aerodimanicas on a 250 GT SWB chassis.

Sold at Bonhams Quail Lodge Auction, Carmel, August 2014, for $6,875,000.

1962
FERRARI *250 GTO*
BERLINETTA

The year it debuted, it completely decimated the competition. There was simply nothing that could compete.

The legendary Ferrari GTO needs little introduction as entire books have been written on this very model alone. It is the most famous, race winning, World Championship-winning, street useable, not to mention achingly beautiful, two-seat coupe from the greatest sporting marque of them all.

Ferrari's Gran Turismo Omologato, or homologated grand tourer, was developed to contest the 3-liter class of the 1962 FIA GT World Championship series of endurance racing events. Development was begun by chief engineer Giotto Bizzarrini using a standard 250 GT short-wheelbase chassis and a race-proven type 168/62 engine from the Testa Rossa as its basis.

The GTO's distinctive front end, with its long, narrowing nose, small radiator inlet, and unique air intakes with removable covers, was the result of a need to reduce drag and, ultimately, increase speed and performance. To help accomplish this, the hood was lengthened and lowered and the engine moved back and placed lower in the chassis to improve weight distribution, which, by extension, improved handling. To further reduce lift and increase stability, a rear spoiler was added as was a spoiler underneath the car formed by the fuel tank cover.

The evocative body created by Scaglietti was made of lightweight aluminum covering the oval-tube frame, which was strengthened for torsional rigidity. The all-alloy, three-liter, twelve-cylinder engine with dry sump lubrication was coupled to a new five-speed synchromesh gearbox. Fitted with six 38DCN Weber carburetors, the engine was able to produce 300 bhp and a top speed of 174 mph.

Inside, the car was simple, owing to its racing purpose, but was nonetheless practical albeit devoid of creature

comforts. Interestingly, the gearshift appeared with an exposed metal gate to define the shift pattern and became thereafter an iconic Ferrari tradition.

Most impressive of all, however, were the results that followed. The year it debuted, the GTO completely decimated the competition to the point that Jaguar, Aston Martin, and Chevrolet all reportedly appealed to the racing governing body with the contention that the GTO was not a true GT car. It was to no avail. Ferrari's world-beater went on to win back-to-back FIA World Championship titles in 1962, 1963, and 1964. Its string of international victories included the Tour de France in 1963 and 1964; class wins in the Targa Florio in 1962, 1963 and 1964; class wins at Le Mans in 1962, and 1963; the Tourist Trophy at Goodwood in 1962 and 1963; and class wins at the Nürburgring 1000 km in 1963 and 1964. There was simply nothing that could compete.

Of these first body types, referred to as Series I, only 31 examples exist in their original form, with just 28 of those

retaining the original 3-liter V12 engines—this car being one of them.

As the car many regard as the ultimate expression of Ferrari, the GTO has achieved legendary status. For aficionados and collectors, it meets all the criteria of desirability: limited production numbers, tremendous racing success, dual-purpose (road and track) functionality, and timeless design. In short, it is nearly perfection personified. And as a result of it being so desirable yet so rare, the Ferrari GTO has recently become the most expensive car in the world. As one noted collector remarked, "For the same price I could own a Van Gogh to hang on the wall. Instead, I get to own an artwork just as beautiful that I can also drive."

It meets all the criteria of desirability:
limited production numbers,
tremendous racing success, dual-purpose
functionality, and timeless design.
In short, it is nearly perfection personified.

FERRARI 250 GTO
BERLINETTA

Coachwork by Scaglietti.

Engine:	2953 cc, 12-cylinder	**Chassis no.:**	3851GT	
Horsepower:	300	**Engine no.:**	3851GT	

Sold at Bonhams Quail Lodge Auction, Carmel, August 2014, for $38,115,000—a world record for any car sold at auction.

1962
MASERATI *TIPO 151*
SPORTS-RACING BERLINETTA

Charismatic, competitive, beautifully designed, and quintessentially Italian, Maserati represented the best of mid-century sporting virtues.

Under the ownership of Adolfo Orsi, Maserati reached what many consider its design zenith. During the late 1930s and, after the second World War, the 1940s through the 1960s, Maserati produced masterful and memorable cars that won races and hearts in spite of being in the shadow of the giant across town—Ferrari. Charismatic, competitive, beautifully designed, and quintessentially Italian, Maserati represented the best of mid-century sporting virtues.

Like many models from the great sporting marques, the Maserati Tipo 151 was built specifically for racing and developed under the Fédération Internationale de l'Automobile (FIA) governing body regulations. While the smaller, more complex, and more successful Tipo 61 "Birdcage" is the most famous Maserati racer of this period, the 151 was no minor achievement.

Essentially an experimental car, the 151 was created using existing Maserati components. Without the budgets of, say, Ferrari or Ford, Maserati had to make due with what it had, owing to its ingenuity and resourcefulness.

Larger and more traditional than the 61, the steel-tube chassis of the 151 was derived from the 450S, while the engine, which also used the 450S as its basis, was uniquely developed to meet the maximum four-liter engine capacity requirements of the new competition class. This new class, World Challenge for Speed and Endurance, was open to all cars entered in the Grand Tourer, Prototype, and Experimental categories with engine sizes between 700 cc–4000 cc. It offered Maserati a fresh opportunity since the traditional GT class required a manufacturer to build 100 production models of a homologated racer, something that was just not possible at the time for Maserati. With this new prospect to still compete in the most prestigious events and maintain their racing image, French and American Maserati importers, Johnny Simone and Briggs Cunningham, respectively, clamored for a suitable contender.

When entered in that year's 24 Hours of Le Mans, the three new 151s ran fast and strong in the opening stages

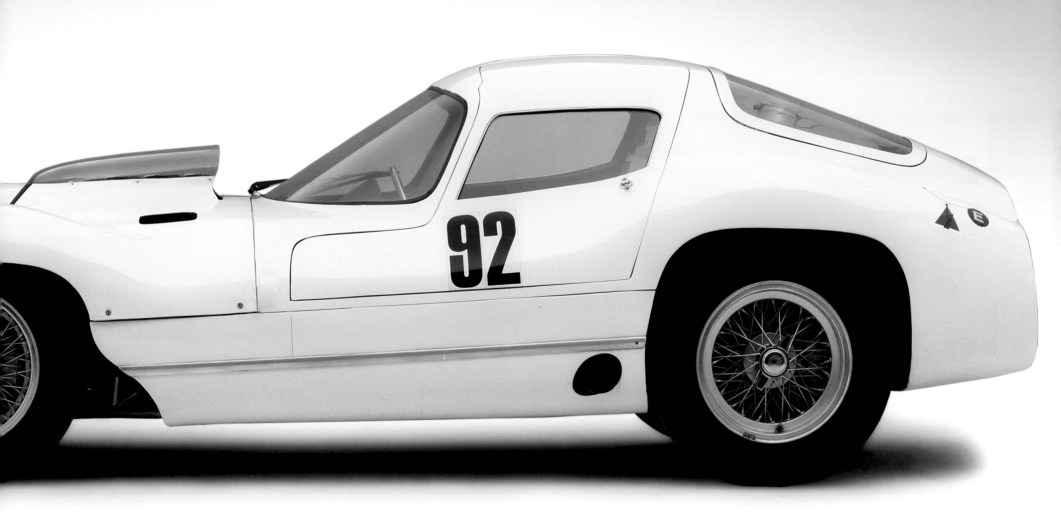

against the very finest entries from Ferrari and Aston Martin, even leading the pack at one point. Unfortunately, each of the 151s had to retire early due to mechanical-related issues. While never champions, the 151 achieved Maserati's ambition of contending world titles and helping sell showroom models to the general public.

Only three 151s were ever built and this particular car, chassis number 151/006, is the sole complete survivor.

MASERATI TIPO 151
SPORTS-RACING BERLINETTA

Coachwork by Allegretti & Gentilini. Ordered and raced by the Briggs Cunningham team at Le Mans.

Engine: 4.4-liter, 8-cylinder   **Chassis no.:** 151/006

Horse Power: 360

Sold at Bonhams Ferrari & Maserati Sale, Gstaad, December 2006, for CHF 2,046,096.

1963

SHELBY *AC COBRA*

260 ROADSTER

"Very simply stated, the Cobra attained higher performance figures than any other production automobile we have tested. And it did it with the 'street' engine."

– *Car and Driver*

The story is well known. Texas farmer turned race car driver and builder, Carroll Shelby, determined that a massive engine crammed into a lightweight body would produce impressive results. And so right he was.

With AC Cars providing the body and Ford providing the horsepower, the Anglo-American effort resulted in what would become the all-conquering Cobra.

Using AC's Ace sports car as the basis and Ford's newly developed 4.3-liter V8 engine, the first Cobras, primarily called AC Cobra in Europe and Shelby Cobra in America, impressed even the most skeptical of critics and garnered shining praise from the media.

Although such a simple concept may seem elementary today, at the time it was revolutionary. When it was introduced, the Cobra had a 1-ton (907 kg) weight savings advantage over the Chevrolet Corvette, America's de facto sports car of the period. To pair a lightweight British chassis and body with a strong, powerful American engine and transmission—with no small effort of customization by a team of California hot rodders employed by Shelby—was tremendously innovative.

In the March 1963 issue of *Car and Driver*, the magazine reviewed the Cobra and used this very car as its test model. The headline read, "AC Cobra—The AC chassis

gets a 4261 cc dose of just exactly what it's always needed." Clearly appreciating the qualities of this new entrant into the automotive industry, *Car and Driver*'s review can be summed up in one of their closing paragraphs: "Very simply stated, the AC Cobra attained higher performance figures than any other production automobile we have tested. And it did it with the 'street' engine."

While the later, enormously powered, 7-liter model that knocked the crown off Ferrari deservedly gets most attention, the early models were anything but pushovers. Surprisingly though, the AC Cobra was a commercial failure despite its success on the track and the enterprise was shuttered by Shelby and Ford in 1967.

This specific car, chassis number CSX2034, has remained in the exact same condition as when *Car and Driver* test drove it. Stored for most of its life, the car is completely original and unaltered, and is a rare and historical representation of the marque that once put America on top of the world.

SHELBY AC COBRA 260 ROADSTER

Cachwork by AC. The Car and Driver test model.

Engine:	4.3-liter, 8-cylinder	**Chassis no.:**	CSX2034
Horsepower:	260		

Sold at Bonhams Quail Lodge Auction, Carmel, August 2013, for $2,068,000.

1961
AUSTIN MINI
COOPER
1275 S COMPETITION

"Stylists are employed to make things obsolescent ... I design cars which cannot be obsolescent and therefore give value ..."

– Alec Issigonis

With its origins based in the fuel shortage period caused by the Suez Crisis of 1956, the most surprising and pleasing feature of the Mini was all the room it afforded as a result of its front-wheel drive layout, which allows 80 percent of the car's floor plan to be used for passengers and luggage. While it may have been frugal with fuel and miniature in size, the Mini delivered bigger than expected results.

What started as a small economy car made by British Motor Corporation (BMC) in 1959 has become such an icon and pervasive part of automotive history and culture that it was voted the second most influential car of the twentieth century.

Designed by Alec Issigonis, the car was initially marketed under BMC's Austin and Morris marques, with Mini becoming its own marque later in 1969 after a decade of overwhelmingly positive reception.

Issigonis' friend John Cooper, owner of the Cooper Car Company and builder of Formula 1 cars (most notably Cooper-Climax) and rally cars, saw the competition potential and collaborated to develop the Mini Cooper. Given

While it may have been frugal with fuel and miniature in size, the Mini delivered bigger than expected results.

a larger capacity, race-tuned engine, along with a closer ratio gearbox and disc brakes—all but non-existent for a car this size at the time—the Mini Cooper opened up a completely new segment for BMC and the British automotive scene.

Two years later in 1963, the Mini Cooper S model was introduced, which was a sportier version of the standard Mini Cooper. As a result of promising outcomes and initial successes in racing, BMC dedicated resources to building specially prepared Minis, mostly based on the Cooper S, to compete in international rallies. Soon Mini Cooper was racking up an impressive list of victories, the most prestigious of which included winning the Monte Carlo Rally an astounding four times. However, Minis also clinched victories in rallies all over the world, including Rally Isle of Man, Circuit of Ireland Rally, Scottish Rally, Rally Sweden, Finnish

1000 Lakes Rally, Rally Poland, Greek Acropolis Rally, and the French Coupes des Alpes rally, among many others.

With its adorable styling, relative roominess, economic efficiency, exciting performance, and go-kart-like handling, the Mini Cooper was a hit.

This particular competition S model was ordered new as a daily driver but went on to race aggressively in Great Britain, Belgium, and France. In the last decade and a half alone, the car has entered a total of 50 races resulting in 26 wins, 13 podium placements, and 16 fastest laps, including winning both the Historic Sports Car Club championship and the Historic Racing Saloon Register championship four times.

AUSTIN MINI COOPER
1275 S COMPETITION

4-time HSCC championship winner and
4-time HRSR championship winner.

Engine:	1275 cc, 4-cylinder	**Chassis no.:**	CA287551918
Horsepower:	78	**Engine no.:**	9FDSA731962

Sold at Bonhams Goodwood Revival Sale, Chichester, September 2014, for £85,500.

1964
PORSCHE *904 GTS*

ENDURANCE RACING COUPE

*"Form has to follow function...
If you analyze the function of an object,
its form often becomes obvious."*

– F. A. "Bützi" Porsche

No medium-capacity Grand Touring car design better embodies the spirit of private-owner endurance racing in the mid-1960s than the pert and legendarily, "user-friendly", four-cylinder, air-cooled Porsche 904 GTS.

The model was Porsche's first foray into fiberglass bodies, which were bonded to a tubular frame chassis with a mid-engine layout. Meant, like all true GTs, to be a dual-purpose car, in practice the 904 saw most use on the track, with excellent performances in the Nürburgring

1000 kms, the Targa Florio, and the 24 Hours of Le Mans.

Very distinct in appearance and a clear departure from the organic evolution of what had become the instantly recognizable Porsche look, the new 904 was like a razor whose aerodynamic form advertised speed. As a true Porsche though, the 904 was endowed with the marque's qualities of performance, reliability, and beauty.

Bought new by famous Swiss racing team owner Georges Filipinetti, this specific 904 was entered by his Scuderia Filipinetti in that year's Nürburgring 1000 km and came in second in class and an extremely impressive sixth overall. When one considers that the five cars that finished ahead of it were all either factory-entered Porsches, Ferraris, or

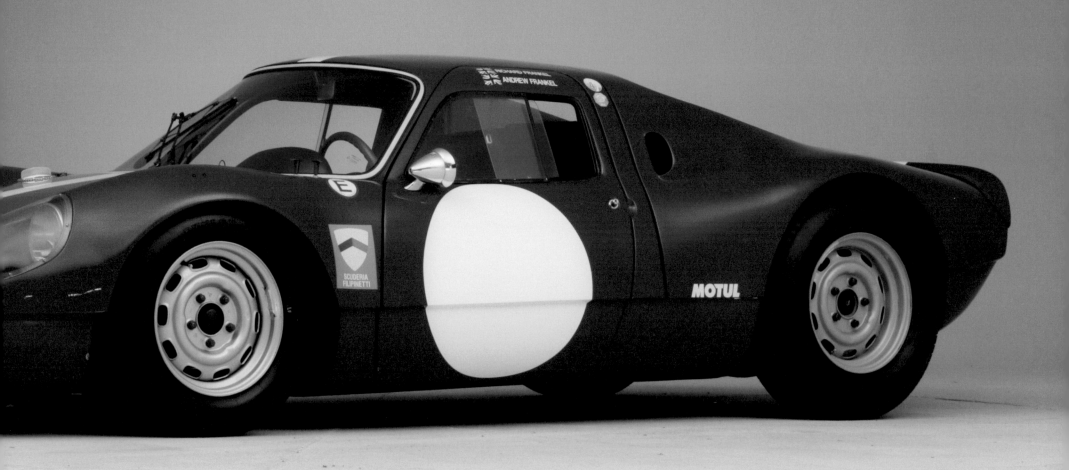

The new 904 was like a razor whose aerodynamic form advertised speed.

privateer Ferrari GTOs boasting 12-cylinder engines, then the accomplishment is clear.

The team then went on to race this car at Le Mans and Reims, among other races, with respectable results, as well as several grueling hill climbs where it also did well.

To stay competitive in ensuing years, the car's original engine was upgraded to a six-cylinder 906 and after initial retirement, graced the Porsche Museum for over two decades, displayed as the ideal example of a privateer 904.

PORSCHE 904 GTS
ENDURANCE RACING COUPE

Raced at Le Mans, Nürburgring,
and Reims, among others.

Engine:	1966 cc, 4-cylinder	**Chassis no.:**	904 079	Sold at Bonhams December Sale, London,
Horse Power:	180	**Engine no.:**	99071/99019	December 2013, for £1,145,000.

1966
FORD *GT40*

Built for one purpose—to beat Ferrari—the GT40 won an astonishing four consecutive Le Mans victories. It was simply the best long-distance race car in the world.

Born from the famous rivalry between Ford and Ferrari, the glorious GT40 was Ford's first car to clinch total victory at the ever-significant 24 Hours of Le Mans. The story of the no-expense-spared GT40 is often repeated, not to mention legendary, owing to the personalities, vast resources, and reputations involved, not to mention the prize.

Built exclusively to beat Ferrari, the first GT40—whose name signifies a Grand Tourer with an overall height of 40 inches—debuted in 1964, but it was not until the magical year of 1966 that it became the world champion it was intended to be. Beginning with that year, the GT40 went on to win an astonishing four consecutive Le Mans victories, as well as four World Sportscar Championship titles.

During those years it was simply the best long-distance race car in the world.

This particular GT40, chassis number 1033, was ordered new by Georges Filipinetti, owner of Switzerland's celebrated Scuderia Filipinetti team. After it was shown at the Geneva Auto Show, it went on to race in a number of important events, including the Monza 1000 and Hockenheim 300, and achieved respectable results. Driven as its maker intended, the Filipinetti GT40 was campaigned widely and earnestly, and no doubt would have made Henry Ford smile.

The significance of the Ford GT40 as one of the most important GTs in history lies not just in the fact that it was a multi-champion. It also demonstrated the ability of American talent and, perhaps more importantly, that a heavy car (weighing 2450 lbs [1111 kg]) with a large-displacement engine could the exact the right formula.

*In the magical year of 1966 it became the
world champion it was intended to be and won
four consecutive Le Mans victories, as well as
four World Sportscar Championship titles.*

FORD GT40

Engine: 4.7-liter, 8-cylinder **Chassis no.:** GT40P/1033

Horse Power: 485

The Geneva Auto Show car. Raced at Monza, Hockenheim, Buenos Aires, and more.

Sold at Bonhams Quail Lodge Auction, Carmel, August 2012, for $2,205,000.

1966
FERRARI *275 GTB/C*

"The 275 GTB/C remains one of the most beautiful Ferraris ever created. It's stunning to look at from any angle and, to many, it represents the perfect embodiment of the 1960s sports car, be it dressed in a road-legal tuxedo or a race-ready suit."

– *Top Gear*

From the day it was delivered new to the castle-dwelling race team owner Georges Filipinetti of Geneva, this automobile, chassis number 09079, has had a fascinating and well-documented history. The eleventh of just twelve built, it became one of the most prominent of those twelve by doing what its makers intended: race and win.

Race-winning cars from Ferrari are not uncommon, but they are so very special. After all, building to race and racing to win was the sole purpose of Ferrari's existence.

This particular car, a 1966 Ferrari 275 Gran Turismo Berlinetta Competizione, or simply 275 GTB/C, is one of those special machines. Under the famous private Swiss team of Scuderia Filipinetti, it won its class at the 1967 24 Hours of Le Mans, 1969 Spa-Francorchamps 1000 km and 1969 Imola 500 km.

Competing three times consecutively in the most prestigious race of them all, Le Mans, in 1967, 1968, and 1969, it won the GT class its first year with Filipinetti team drivers Rico Steinmann and Dieter Spörry. Then in 1969, the first and only time it raced Spa-Francorchamps, it won that GT class with Filipinetti team drivers Jacques Rey and Edgar Berney, and then went on to win its class at Imola. In the right hands, number 09079 was a force to be reckoned with.

Launched in 1966, this new GT-class Ferrari designed expressly for competition was built around a completely new chassis specific to this model. It was lighter and stronger than the chassis of the standard 275, was fitted with reinforced wheel hubs and wider than standard wheels, and given twin saddle-mounted alloy fuel tanks with quick-access exterior fuel and oil filler caps. Additionally, it was wrapped in an ultra-thin alloy body thereby reducing weight even further.

The powerplant was also new, with a Tipo 213 Competition motor developed from the Ferrari factory team racer campaigned the previous year. The new 3.3-liter, V12 engine with fully dry sump benefited from a long list of uprated factory modifications. The strategic placement of this stirring engine—lower and further back—also provided more advantage with its nearly per-

fect weight distribution.

Not only were the physical properties of this car quite impressive but the aesthetics also wowed the world. Its long, shark-like nose with gill-like side vents and low, wide stance made it appear both handsome and predatory at once. And its practicality, too, made it enormously attractive as it could be ferociously raced on the track or sportingly driven to the country club.

After its tenure with Filipinetti, car 09079 found a home with several American collections during the 1970s and 80s. Then in 1985, its body was severely damaged in a

Race—winning cars from Ferrari are not uncommon but they are so very special. After all, building to race and racing to win was the sole purpose of Ferrari's existence.

garage fire but the engine, drive train, and chassis remained intact. The car was shipped to Italy, where its bodywork was meticulously and accurately restored to factory specifications by marque experts Carrozzeria Brandoli, after which it received its red book certification from Ferrari Classiche confirming its matching numbers engine, chassis, suspension, and transaxle.

Since then, the laurel-ladened car has won several honors at contemporary and classic events, such as the

The eleventh of just twelve built, it became one of the most prominent of those by doing what its makers intended: race and win.

Pebble Beach Concours d'Elegance, and in 2014 was one of just 60 Ferraris selected worldwide to represent the sixtieth anniversary of Ferrari in Beverly Hills.

FERRARI 275 GTB/C

Coachwork by Scaglietti. 1 of 12 built. Class winner of Le Man, Spa-Francorchamps, and Imola.

Engine:	3286 cc, 12-cylinder	**Chassis no.:**	09079
Horse Power:	320	**Engine no.:**	09079

Sold at Bonhams Scottsdale Auction, Scottsdale, January 2015, for $9,405,000—a world auction record for the model.

1967
ISO *GRIFO*
5.4-LITER COUPE

"Proof that pedigree doesn't mean a thing. The new Iso Grifo is sitting where it belongs—at the head of the table."

– *Car and Driver*

The Grifo by Iso was a GT automobile comprising American power and Italian style. Sporty and luxurious, it was the polar opposite of Iso's earlier product, the adorable Isetta micro car.

Powered by a Chevrolet 5.4-liter, V8 engine producing 350 horsepower and a top speed of more than 150 mph—with later models receiving even larger engines, the Grifo was very much a potent car meant to compete with other Italian GTs of the period, namely Ferrari and Maserati.

Designed in concert with Giotto Bizzarrini (of Ferrari GTO fame and later his own eponymous marque) and Bertone coachbuilders' Giorgio Giugiaro (responsible for the Maserati Ghibli and De Tomaso Mangusta, among many others), the Grifo received praiseworthy reviews from automotive media but never the same level of enthusiasm from customers. Despite its strong performance, beautifully appointed interior and favorable price, economic success eluded the Grifo and only 400-some examples of the coupe were ever produced.

Impressive, distinct, and uncommon, the short life of the Iso Grifo belies its great legacy.

"As a comfortable GT machine the Iso is an unqualified success…A very rewarding car for the skillful."

– Car and Driver

"Its Giugiaro styling brings people to their knees."

– Automobile

ISO GRIFO 5.4-LITER COUPE

Coachwork by Bertone.

Engine: 5359 cc, 8-cylinder
Horse Power: 320

Chassis no.: GL730138D
Engine no.: 823-F 12125P

Sold at Bonhams Goodwood Festival of Speed Sale, Chichester, June 2014, for £191,900.

1967
MASERATI *GHIBLI*
4.7-LITER COUPE

"Blame the Ghibli for completely warping our standards for automotive aesthetics since most cars sitting next to it look like cinder blocks... In beauty, the Ghibli...reigns."

– Car and Driver

Maserati debuted the Ghibli in coupe form at the Turin Motor Show in late 1966. Styled at Carrozzeria Ghia by the talented Giorgetto Giugiaro and named after the hot, southwesterly wind from the Sahara Desert, the Ghibli rivaled the Ferrari Daytona for straight performance while beating it in price. Long and sleek, it had a robust, aerodynamic appearance that made quite an impression.

Of the design, *Car and Driver* said, "...Blame the Ghibli for completely warping our standards for automotive aesthetics since most cars sitting next to it look like cinder blocks." Adding, "In beauty, the Ghibli...reigns."

Not just endowed with beauty but also brawn, the Ghibli's power unit was the four-camshaft, 90-degree V8, an engine derived from Maserati's 450 S sports racer and first seen in road-going guise in the 5000 GT. Performance was in the form of neck-snapping acceleration that resulted from enormous torque. The Ghibli may have been heavy (with a curb weight of 3637 lbs [1650 kgs]) but was powerful, and top speeds could reach nearly 170 mph.

This particular car, chassis number AM115.090, was bought new by country singer and songwriter Bobbie Gentry. Her famous single *Ode to Billie Joe* had hit the top of the charts that same year, and with the proceeds

she bought herself the Ghibli. Two years later, Gentry married casino mogul and famed car collector Bill Harrah, wherein the Maserati no doubt found good company.

"It takes just one look to understand why the Maserati Ghibli outsold both the Ferrari Daytona and the Lamborghini Miura."

– Motor Trend

*"That gorgeous Giugiaro
bodywork and that famed V8
engine deserve our respect."*

– Road & Track

MASERATI GHIBLI
4.7-LITER COUPE

Coachwork by Ghia.

Sold at Bonhams Quail Lodge Auction, Carmel, August 2014, for $385,000.

Engine:	4719 cc, 8-cylinder	**Chassis no.:**	AM115.090
Horsepower:	330	**Engine no.:**	AM115.090

PORSCHE *908.02*

FACTORY RACING SPORTS PROTOTYPE "FLUNDER" LANGHECK SPYDER

---

*After having found its stride,
the 908.02 went on to successes …
annihilating the competition!*

Introduced in 1968, the Typ 908 was the successor to the 907 in Porsche's racing evolution. Although that year's racing calendar became dedicated to resolving various teething issues with the new model, the resulting "version 2.0"—the 908.02—was nearly flawless.

Whereas the original 908 was a closed coupe, the 908.02 featured an open top spyder configuration. With the roof removed, the car was around 200 lbs (91 kg) lighter, which helped it gain considerably more horsepower. To compensate in aerodynamics, Porsche updated the fiberglass body with a sleeker profile that included a cleaner nose, smaller air intake, flattened wheel arches, higher waistline, and a more tightly enclosed cockpit. While the media dubbed the new look the *flunder*—flounder in German—for its flat, fish-like appearance, the car was super lightweight, fast, and extremely nimble.

After having finally found its stride at the Brands Hatch 1000 km where the model finished 1-2-3, defeating even the Ferrari 312P, the 908.02 went on to successes at Monza, Spa, the Targa Florio, and, especially, Nürburgring, where 908s finished 1-2-3-4-5, annihilating the competition!

This particular car, chassis number 02-05, was raced extensively worldwide, including at Sebring, Monza, Targa Florio, Spa, Nürburgring, Watkins Glen, and Buenos Aires. At the 1970 12 Hours of Sebring the car raced alongside

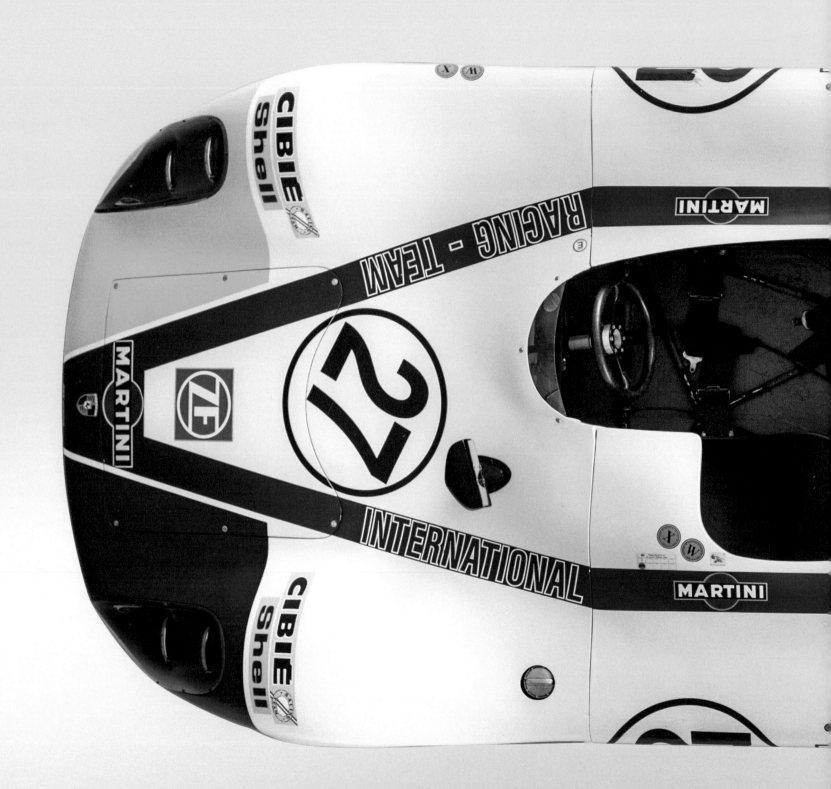

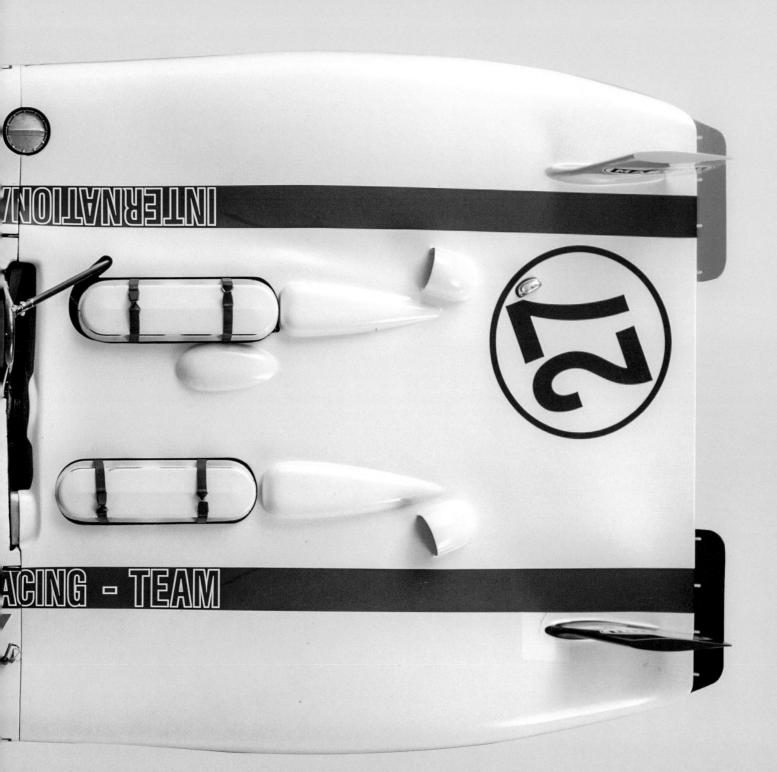

Peter Revson and Steve McQueen in their 908.02 in what was certainly one of the most exciting races in Sebring history. With just minutes left in the race, the Revson/McQueen Porsche was in an all out battle for first place with the much larger Ferrari 512 of Mario Andretti and Arturo Merzario. Ultimately, the Ferrari won the day, but the Porsche clinched second place just 23 seconds behind the victor—all with McQueen's broken foot still in a cast. The highlight for this car, however, was when it was driven later that season to third place at the 24 Hours of Le Mans by Helmut Marko and Rudi Lins, helping Porsche clinch a 1-2-3 whitewash at the world's most prestigious endurance race.

Although it took time to hone, the German engineering team at Porsche, led by Ferdinand Piëch, persevered and after refinement upon refinement finally found a winning formula in the Typ 908.02, taking home a well deserved 1969 World Championship of Makes title.

While the media dubbed the new look the flunder—*flounder in German*—for its flat, fish-like appearance, the car was super lightweight, fast, and extremely nimble.

PORSCHE 908.02 FACTORY RACING SPORTS PROTOTYPE "FLUNDER" LANGHECK SPYDER AEROCOUPER

Engine:	2990 cc, 8-cylinder	**Chassis no.:**	908/02-05
Horsepower:	350		

3rd place winner at Le Mans; also raced at Monza, Spa, Nürburgring, and more. Driven by Vic Elford at Sebring and Targa Florio.

Sold at Bonhams Bond Street Sale, London, November 2014, for £2,185,500.

1970
—
1997

1970
DE TOMASO
MANGUSTA
COUPE

*With awing performance,
the Mangusta is a rare example
of the dawn of the supercar.*

One of the very first supercars, the Mangusta effectively established De Tomaso as a serious automobile manufacturer on its arrival in 1967.

Alejandro de Tomaso had begun racing in his native Argentina before moving to Italy to drive for Maserati and OSCA. Inspired by the Maserati brothers and the automotive greenhouse that was Modena at the time, he decided to form his own company, De Tomaso Automobili, in 1959.

Beginning by building racing cars for Formula Junior, 1, 2, and 3, the De Tomaso company did not create its first road car, the Vallelunga, until several years later. While this mid-engined coupe was not a success, it did help De Tomaso form the basis of the forthcoming Mangusta.

Styled by Carrozzeria Ghia's Giorgetto Giugiaro (responsible for the Aston Martin DB4 GT Jet, Maserati Ghibli, and Iso Grifo, among many others), the car's design is very appropriate for the brute it clothed. Employing the same engine Ford used to power their GT40 Le Mans challenger, a 289 cubic inch V8, the Mangusta (mongoose in Italian) could deliver more than 300 horsepower with speeds exceeding 150 mph, while disc brakes helped restrain the awing performance.

With just 401 examples produced from 1967 until 1972 and only around 250 still in existence, the Mangusta is a rare example of the dawn of the supercar.

*"A true icon of
automotive design."*

- Racecar

DE TOMASO MANGUSTA COUPE

Coachwork by Ghia.

Engine: 4736 cc, 8-cylinder   **Chassis no.:** 8MA-1216   Sold at Bonhams December Sale, London, December 2013, for £203,100.

Horsepower: 306

1970
MONTEVERDI
HAI 450 SS
COUPE

Built to exact revenge ... the car sneaked upon the automotive world like its namesake and made a sensational splash.

Not all supercars came from Italy. Unlikely as it may seem, the idyllic land of cuckoo clocks and chocolate also produced an impressive model of automobile exotica—the Monteverdi Hai.

Thanks to Enzo Ferrari's famously controversial personality, there may have never been a Bizzarrini, Lamborghini, or, in this case, a Monteverdi. Peter Monteverdi was the Ferrari importer for Switzerland and after a famous falling out with *il Commendatore* decided to exact revenge by building his own car.

Introducing the Hai (shark in German) at the 1970 Geneva Auto Show, the car sneaked up on the automotive world like its namesake and made a sensational splash. "It was the unquestionable star of the show,"

recalled Monteverdi executive Paul Berger. "All the newspapers came to our stand, as did the president of the Swiss Confederation, and *Automobil Revue* put it on their cover."

Similar to Iso Grifo and De Tomaso, Monteverdi used an American powerplant. In this case it was the Chrysler 7.2-liter V8, which was straightforward, reliable, and, most of all, mighty. All told, the Hai produced an incredible 450 bhp with a top speed of nearly 170 mph.

With an avant-garde design executed by Fissore coachbuilders, the Hai was built on a sturdy tubular chassis and handled very well owing to excellent weight distribution and thoughtful rear suspension. The interiors were plush and the craftsmanship worthy of Swiss standards. The attention-grabbing supercar exuded power, elegance, and speed, and was extremely alluring.

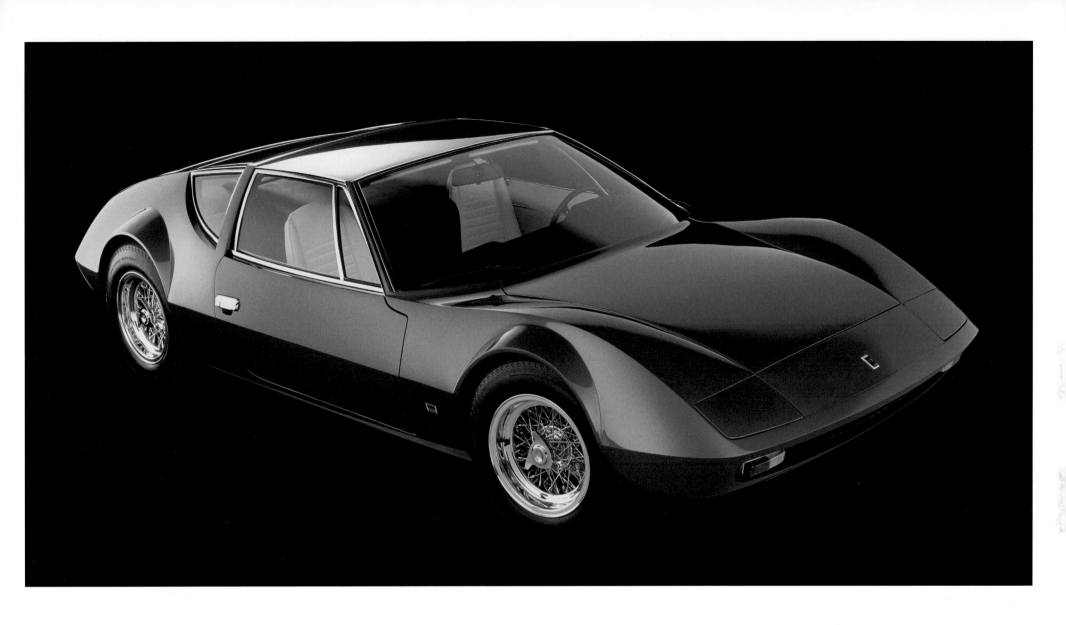

"Then there is the soundtrack. When the revs rise and the mechanics of the engine are drowned by the noise of its efforts, the glorious V8 cacophony is so close you might be listening to it through Sennheisers (headphones). And above all else is the sheer brutality of it. With confidence ... the Hai propels with immense force, the tires feeling as if they are grinding down the tarmac as it shreds through the gears. Absolutely, uniquely awe-inspiring."

- Classic & Sports Car

Initially, the car gained the impression of being "unavailable" to the general public with owners having to be vetted due to the high performance nature of the Hai, regardless if they could afford the price. While this was not the case, the publicity-savvy Mr. Monteverdi did not explicitly correct this rumor, as it only created buzz and built up the image of extreme performance and exclusivity. Unfortunately, with the oil crisis of 1973 the market for the Hai, as with all cars of its class, was immediately devastated.

This specific car was the very first Hai created, the one that wowed audiences at the Geneva Motor Show, and the car that was subsequently tested by the media to enthusiastic reviews.

MONTEVERDI HAI L450 SS COUPE

Coachwork by Fissore. The first Hai made and the Geneva Motor Show car.

Engine:	4.7-liter, 8-cylinder	Chassis no.:	TNT 101
Horsepower:	450	Engine no.:	MN 426310070471

Sold at Bonhams Rétromobile Sale, Paris, January 2010, for €398,000.

1970
PORSCHE *917*
COUPE/SPYDER

"To John Wyer of JW Automotive Engineering fame, it was the future of motorsport; to race anything against the 917 would be defeat. 'Porsche had, typically, done it first,' Wyer mused, 'and at a stroke, every other car was out of date.'"

– Autoweek

T he 917 was Porsche's first 12-cylinder car as well as the first car to give the German marque its first overall victory at the 24 Hours of Le Mans. Appearing in a number of iterations over the course of its competitive life, the 917 also gained notoriety in popular culture as Steve McQueen's charger in the movie *Le Mans*.

This 917 model, while now configured as a 917 Spyder, began life as a 917K Coupe ("K" representing kurzheck or

short tail in German) sporting the illustrious blue-and-orange Gulf Oil racing livery. It was campaigned new at Le Mans in 1970 by David Hobbs and multiple World Championship-winning motorcycle racer Mike Hailwood. During the race, Hailwood hydroplaned in the rain and crashed heavily, ending a promising opportunity for a podium placement. Unharmed, he walked back to the pits carrying the steering wheel where he was reputedly greeted by the team's famously uninviting principal, John Wyer, who dryly said, "Hello Michael, is that what caused it or is that all that's left?"

As was customary and well documented, Porsche took the car and rebuilt it using a new chassis, number 031. Later in 1972, the car was reconfigured into the Spyder

917s were not just the stars in Steve McQueen's movie Le Mans, *they were stars on the track, delivering Porsche its first overall victory at* Le Mans.

form that it wears today. All the while, the car was campaigned at circuits such as Nürburgring, Imola, Silverstone, Hockenheim, Nuremburg, and many more. Such was the common, constantly modifying, always bettering nature of international high stakes racing.

Representing an extraordinary era of motor racing and a high-water mark for Porsche, this battle-tested, provenance-rich 917 is an excellent example of what is often regarded as one of the greatest racing cars of all time.

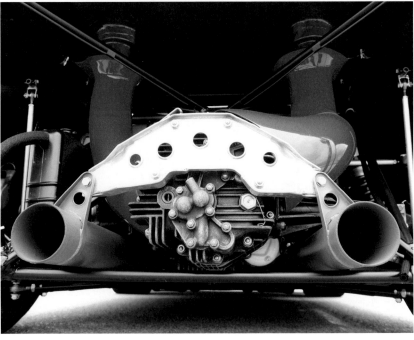

PORSCHE LE MANS 917K COUPE / 1972
INTERSERIE 917 SPYDER

Engine:	4494 cc, 12-cylinder	**Chassis no.:**	917 026
Horsepower:	580	**Engine no.:**	917 031

Porsche's first 12-cylinder model Raced at Le Mans, Silverstone, Imola, and more.

Sold at Bonhams Quail Lodge Auction, Carmel, August 2010, for $3,967,000—a world record for the marque.

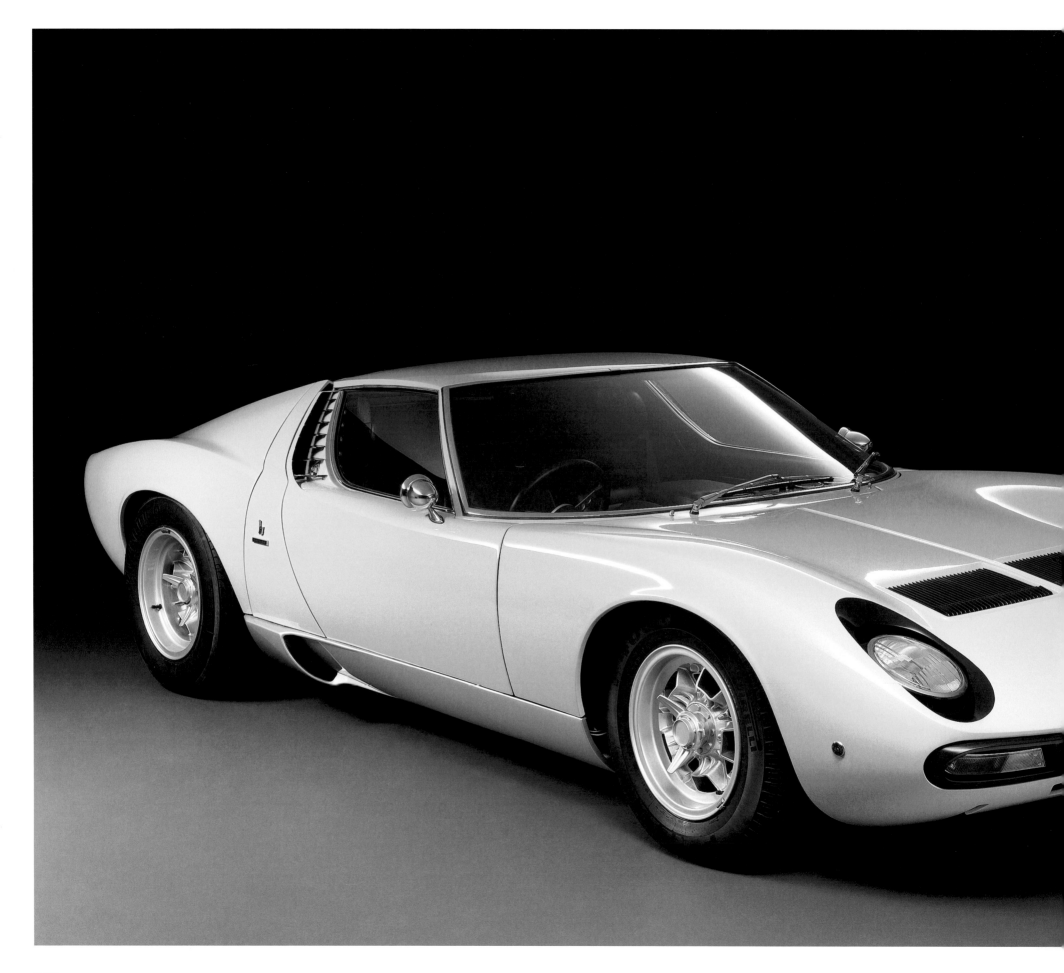

1972

LAMBORGHINI
MIURA SV

COUPE

> *"The Miura pretty well set the whole motoring world on its ear."*
>
> *– Road & Track*

The turbulent milieu of the mid-1960s served as a backdrop for an escalating battle between two ambitious Italian figureheads: Enzo Ferrari (the establishment) and Ferruccio Lamborghini (the feisty upstart). Lamborghini's elegant 350 GT challenged Ferrari's prevailing designs in 1964, but Ferruccio's boundary-pushing hubris did not fully emerge until the former tractor builder revealed a rolling chassis of his Miura concept at the 1965 Turin Salon and the complete production version at Geneva the following year.

The Miura would later earn the unofficial moniker of being the world's first supercar for good reason: not only were its slinky bodywork and eyelash'd headlights like nothing the world had seen before, its mechanical underpinnings also revealed an equally arresting amount of brawn, complexity, and innovation. More importantly, the Miura staked its claim as the world's fastest production car, triggering an arms race for ultimate horsepower, acceleration, and top speed.

Named after legendary bull breeder Don Eduardo Miura Fernández, Lamborghini's creation boasted a groundbreaking combination of elegant form and aggressive function when it debuted on the world stage. The chassis engineering and vehicle dynamics were overseen by the legendary Gian Paolo Dallara, who later left Lamborghini to form Dallara Automobili, which later became a major force in Formula 3, Formula 1, and IndyCar racing. Nestled beneath Carrozzeria Bertone's sensuous aluminum skin (designed by Marcello Gandini) was a transversely mounted 4.0-liter V12 producing 350 hp. The powerplant was cloaked behind the car's signature "venetian blind" engine louvers, and was capable of propelling the two-seater to a claimed

top speed of 180 mph, a remarkable figure for the day. Because of the Miura's spaceship-like silhouette, low-slung proportions, and scarcity of space around the V12, novel packaging solutions were necessary to execute Lamborghini's vision, including sharing oil between the engine and gearbox, and housing the transmission and differential within the same aluminum alloy case.

The first of three Miura generations was known as the P400. The P was short for *posteriore*, reflecting the V12's rearward configuration, and the 400 referred to the

"I still miss the Miura. No one has ever equalled it. When I miss the sound and the fury, I take refuge in my garage and turn the key in the ignition of my Miura. Just long enough to make the needle move."

– Ferruccio Lamborghini

engine's 4-liter displacement. The P400 S model was unveiled in 1968 and incorporated decorative trim, various creature comforts, and engine enhancements that added 20 horsepower. The final iteration was the P400 SV (short for *spinto veloce*—signifying tuned fast), which further boosted horsepower to 390 and featured wider fender flares housing bigger wheels and tires, and the deletion of the famous headlight lashes.

This particular Lamborghini SV, chassis number 4818, rolled off the assembly line on May 31, 1972, and was number 701 of the 765 Miuras produced at Lamborghini's Sant'Agata Bolognese headquarters. Purchased new by rock star Rod Stewart, the car was ordered with the rare air conditioning option and an in-dash Phillips radio/cassette unit. It was also equipped with the split sump lubrication system introduced in 1971, which separated the oil reservoirs for the engine and transmission.

Though it served as the ultimate expression of the Miura, only 150 SV variants were produced (out of a total of 765 models) because the announcement of Lamborghini's next flagship, the wedge-shaped Countach, distracted

from the Miura's flowing lines with an even more alien silhouette. Production ceased in late 1972 to make way for the next big-engined Lamborghini, marking the end of the brand's curve-driven design direction.

The Miura would earn the unofficial moniker of being the world's first supercar for good reason … it was like nothing the world had seen before.

LAMBORGHINI MIURA
SV COUPE

Engine:	3929 cc, 12-cylinder	**Chassis no.:**	4818
Horsepower:	385	**Engine no.:**	30734

Coachwork by Bertone. Formerly owned by Rod Stewart

Sold at Bonhams Goodwood Revival Sale, Chichester, September 2013, for £919,900.

1972
LANCIA *STRATOS*
STRADALE

As a trailblazing rally car whose race victories backed up its radical looks, the Stratos proves that brutalist engineering, audacious design, and a singular vision for speed can nudge a car towards greatness.

Jaunty and insect-like, the Lancia Stratos possessed squat proportions, a miniscule wheelbase, and straightedge surfaces that made it seem poised to pounce when it debuted in 1971 at the Turin Motor Show as the Stratos HF concept car. Unlike some performance cars of its era that were powerful but ill-equipped for competition, the Stratos Stradale was a rare example of a road-going vehicle built for the sole purpose of homologation so its race counterpart could exist. As such, Lancia was required to build 500 cars to meet rally racing rules, only 40 of which faced competition.

The Stratos was penned with a sense of hyperbolic sense of exuberance by Marcello Gandini, the Bertone designer who made his name with the outlandish Lamborghini Miura and Countach. In race trim, the Stratos packed a 300 horsepower, 2418 cc Ferrari V6 engine that was plucked from the Dino and mounted amidships. The generous engine output was even more notable because the race version of the Stratos weighed under 2,000 lbs (907 kg); that fearsome power-to-weight ratio combined with notoriously twitchy handling earned this tiny two-seater a reputation as a widow-maker. Though its explosive acceleration and Mercurial ability to swap ends made it difficult to manage, when handled properly, the Stratos was capable of outperforming almost anything on the rally course, as evidenced by its World Rally Championship wins in 1974, 1975, and 1976.

Though its provocative looks cut a distinctive swath on public roads, the street car's impractical underpinnings made the Stratos ill-suited for daily use. The non-race version's V6 produced a relatively modest 192 bhp at 7000 rpm, but the Stratos' extensive use of fiberglass enabled it to weigh under 2200 lbs (998 kg), emboldening it to make the 0-60 mph sprint in under 5 seconds.

Despite its endlessly entertaining driving dynamics, the Stratos Stradale became the automotive equivalent of a white elephant for a number of reasons including its mercilessly tight cabin space, awkward ergonomics, and dubious quality control. But its mechanical backbone and high-strung personality also made it nothing short of legendary. As such, the road-going Stradale was burdened with just enough quirks to leave countless examples languishing in showrooms for years, with some serving as free prizes for well-performing dealerships.

When handled properly, the Stratos was capable of outperforming almost any-thing on the rally course.

It may have been originally designed as a race car first and a road car second, but the Stratos Stradale offers some unexpected amenities for those who dare pilot it on public highways. For starters, the Stradale's windshield offers surprising forward visibility, incorporating a constant radius shape that minimizes distortion. Perhaps that concession almost makes up for the rearward visibility, which is almost nil. Though it barely sits at waist height, the diminutive Stradale manages generous ground clearance in order to minimize bottoming out on rally courses. Keeping in the spirit of its race counterpart, the street-going Stratos features molded door pockets that are capable of holding a helmet. The car's drivetrain is also widely viewed as bulletproof, with a stout platform and the ability to take a lashing from heavy-handed pilots.

As a trailblazing rally car whose race victories backed up its radical looks, the Stratos proves that brutalist engineering, audacious design, and a singular vision for speed can nudge a car towards greatness. One notable byproduct of the Stratos' extreme performance dynamics is the fact that many examples have been lost to wrecks—which, though unfortunate, is also what makes it so desirable.

LANCIA STRATOS STRADALE

Coachwork by Bertone. Unrestored "barn find" condition.

Engine:	2418 cc, 6-cylinder	**Chassis no.:**	829ARO 001941	Sold at Bonhams Quail Lodge Auction, Carmel, August 2013, for $264,000.
Horsepower:	192	**Engine no.:**	12111	

1973
FERRARI *365 GTS/4*
DAYTONA SPIDER

*Fast, beautiful, and unapologetically racy,
it lives as a lasting example of Ferrari's
ability to combine race–bred engineering
with evocative design.*

The romance of racing often informs a manufacturer's sports car offerings, which helps explain why the Ferrari GTB/4 and GTS/4 unofficially earned the Daytona nickname. The reference was a hat tip to the brand's 1-2-3 victory at the Florida raceway in 1967, and the road-going models introduced the following year not only recalled the brand's domination at the famed circuit, they also served as an answer to Lamborghini's burgeoning presence on the exotic car scene.

Though not quite as visually shocking as Lamborghini's Miura, the 365 GTB/4, which debuted at the Paris Salon in 1968, nonetheless imposed a bold, sexy silhouette with an extravagantly elongated nose, a short passenger compartment and an elegantly compact tail. Conceived by Leonardo Fioravanti, the Pininfarina design was both muscular and wistful, serving as a visual counterpoint to its lavishly curvaceous competitor.

The 365's original design featured fixed headlights beneath Perspex housings that were modified with a pop-up-style setup due to US regulations prohibiting covered headlamps. Beneath the 365 GTS/4's expansive snout was a four-cam, 4390 cc V12 producing 352 horsepower at a screaming 7500 rpm, which helped it claim its status as the world's fastest production car at the time. The powerplant's high-revving quality not only offered a sonorous

answer to competitors, it further escalated the era's supercar wars. While some 1400 Berlinetta coupes were built during the car's production run, only 123 Spider convertibles were unleashed on public roads making them not only more rare than their closed coupe counterparts but also considerably more valuable in the four decades since their introduction. That scarcity was notable enough to make the open-air models the object of envy, inspiring many coupe owners to chop their Daytonas and convert them into unauthorized Spiders.

Fast, beautiful, and unapologetically racy, the 365 GTS/4 Daytona Spider lives as a lasting example of Ferrari's ability to combine race-bred engineering with evocative design.

The Daytona nickname was a hat tip to the brand's 1-2-3 victory at the Florida raceway in 1967.

The powerplant's high-revving quality not only offered a sonorous answer to competitors, it further escalated the era's supercar wars.

FERRARI 365 GTS/4
DAYTONA SPIDER

Engine:	4390 cc, 12-cylinder	**Chassis no.:**	17057
Horsepower:	352	**Engine no.:**	B2944

Coachwork by Scaglietti.

Sold at Bonhams Quail Lodge Auction, Carmel, August 2014, for $2,640,000.

PORSCHE *911*

CARRERA RS 2.7

"Good design is honest. A coherently designed product requires no adornment; it should be enhanced by its form alone."

- F.A. "Bützi" Porsche

For the grandson of Porsche paterfamilias Ferdinand Porsche, F.A. Porsche, or Bützi, as he was called, good design was inherent. However, when he first designed what would become the 911, little did he know that it would go on to become the basis of one of the most iconic and successful sports cars in history.

One of the many beautiful things about the 911 is its ability to evolve, artfully and effectively, without compromising its primary form—a form that many consider to be the very definition of functional and aesthetic synergy.

The fact that Porsche's flagship model recently celebrated its golden jubilee demonstrates just how relevant the 911 has remained. To stay fashionable and desirable—not to mention competitive and technologically advanced—is truly astonishing, particularly when the general design has largely remained unchanged. A first-year 911 from over half a century ago is immediately recognizable as the direct ancestor of today's land rocket from Stuttgart. With such unbroken visual as well as practical lineage, no other car can boast such pedigree. In the world of design, timelessness is impossibly rare. In the world of performance design, such a feat is simply unprecedented.

It is from this legacy of accomplishment that the now legendary 911 Carrera RS 2.7 was created. First built in 1973—a decade after the very first 911—specifically for homologation so Porsche could race in the highly competitive FIA Group 4 class (a class which essentially required the car to be the same model consumers could find on the showroom floor), this iteration of the 911 would be handsomely uprated from its elder brethren.

At first glance, the name is a confident expression of Team Porsche's ambitions. Taking *Carrera* (meaning race in

Spanish) from the marque's successive class wins in the gruelling Carrera Panamericana and *Rennsport* (meaning racing in German)—abbreviated to RS—an assertion, even a duelling challenge, was issued through nomenclature.

The flat 6-cylinder, 2.4-liter engine of the already respectably fast 911 S was bored out to 2.7-liters, increasing horsepower to 210 with torque following suit. Stiffer suspension was added, wider rear wheels were mounted with wider rear fenders to accommodate them, and larger brakes were attached. To increase stability at high speed, Porsche engineers added a redesigned front air dam and the now iconic rear "ducktail" spoiler, which this model has not—a rarely exercised factory option referred to as "ducktail delete." And to decrease weight, the car was wrapped with thinner gauge steel, used thinner gauge glass, and sported a spartan interior.

The result were numbers that speak for themselves: 0-60 in 5.6 seconds and a top speed of 150 mph. But most important of all was the effect it achieved on the track.

This tasty combination of attributes, particularly for a car that could be domestically driven around town and then seriously raced on the weekend, made for what is considered today by many the greatest dual-purpose Porsche ever created and surely one of the finest sports cars off all time.

PORSCHE 911
CARRERA RS 2.7

Engine:	2687cc, 6-cylinder	**Chassis no.:**	9113600125
Horsepower:	210	**Engine no.:**	6630156

Desirable "first 500" production Carrera. Rare ducktail-delete option.

Sold at Bonhams Quail Lodge Auction, Carmel, August 2014, for $935,000.

LAMBORGHINI
COUNTACH LP400
"PERISCOPICO" COUPE

Not only did it solidify Lamborghini's reputation as a bold, innovative player on the supercar world stage, it captured the imagination of a generation of enthusiasts, entering a new realm of otherworldly design and blistering performance.

Marcello Gandini joined the pantheon of legendary automotive designers by penning several of the most memorable supercars in history. It could be argued that few, if any, of his competitors' creations appeared on as many boyhood posters as the Lamborghini Countach.

Before the over-the-top Countach iterations of the 1980s, the wedge-shaped Countach LP400 model originated as a simple yet dramatic follow-up to the groundbreaking and more curvaceous Miura, with a massive, flat expanse of a front windshield and a squat stance. Though it carried over the Miura's four-cam, four-liter V12 motor and running gear, the Countach's styling cues indicated a more futurist, angular look that would come to redefine the brand's visual signature.

Designed for Lamborghini by Gandini within Bertone's studio, the first Countach flaunted an aerodynamically optimized shape that managed to combine a low, menacing profile with whimsical wheel arches and a so-called roof-mounted periscope to enable rearward visibility. Side windows were of the half-height variety, lending a lean, squat look. More notably, this was the first Lamborghini to boast upward sweeping scissor doors which added a sense of occasion to the already striking silhouette.

"It's very simple. In the past, I have bought some of the most famous Gran Turismo cars, and in each of these magnificent machines I have found some faults. Too hot. Or uncomfortable. Or not sufficiently fast. Or not perfectly finished. Now I want to make a GT car without faults. Not a technical bomb. Very normal. Very conventional. But a perfect car."

– *Ferruccio Lamborghini*

The wedge-shaped Countach LP400 was the first Lamborghini to boast upward sweeping scissor doors.

Dubbed the LP400 for its longitudinal posterior engine configuration and 4-liter displacement, the V12-powered beast could hit 170 mph yet look every bit as fast while standing still. Though it faced packaging challenges like its Miura predecessor, the Countach's gearbox's positioning between the seats and its rearward differential created superior weight distribution, lending the new model improved balance and more predictable handling.

Devoid of the later models' spoilers and ground effects, the Countach LP400 "Periscopico" represented a futurist sequel to the Miura and an understated predecessor to subsequent Countach variants. Not only did the LP400 solidify Lamborghini's reputation as a bold, innovative player on the supercar world stage, it captured the imagination of a generation of enthusiasts, entering a new realm of otherworldly design and blistering performance.

LAMBORGHINI COUNTACH LP400
'PERISCOPICO' COUPE

Engine:	3929 cc, 12-cylinder	**Chassis no.:**	1120070
Horse Power:	375	**Engine no.:**	1120068

Coachwork by Bertone.

Sold at Bonhams Goodwood Festival of Speed Sale, Chichester, June 2014, for £953,500.

1979
BMW *M1*
PRO-CAR

Both supercar and pop culture artwork, the Frank Stella-painted M1 is the literal definition of 'functional art'—a high-performance and invaluable one at that.

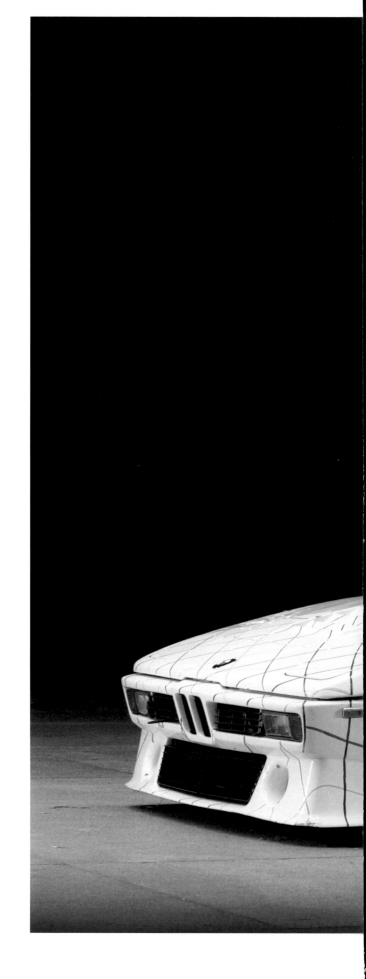

Despite a rich history of engineering innovations and motorsports endeavors, by the mid-1970s BMW assumed an aura of relative conservatism. Because the Munich-based brand lacked a proper supercar in its stable, its sporty coupes and sedans seemed somewhat pedestrian against more daring car makers like Porsche, who actively campaigned circuits like Le Mans with unrelenting race cars.

The answer to the supercar conundrum was to commence development of a new flagship, which was dubbed the M1 and served as the inaugural effort of the newly formed BMW Motorsport GmbH division. Paul Bracq's initial design featured a mid-mounted, 3.5-liter V6 surrounded by a tubular spaceframe chassis wrapped in fiberglass bodywork, boasting a shark-like nose that recalled the brand's heritage while simultaneously pushing the design into the future.

Development work was first contracted to Lamborghini (who later withdrew from the project) and subsequently to ItalDesign, before final work was executed at Karosserie Baur in Stuttgart. BMW set out to create a boundary-pushing exotic car, and to achieve those goals the M1 featured Gianpaolo Dallara's suspension work with a 277 horsepower powerplant that made it the fastest German production car when it debuted in 1978.

Giorgetto Giugiaro's design assumed an aggressive look when modified for race duty with ground effects, flared wheel arches, and a large spoiler. The inline-6 powerplant also enjoyed heavy modifications, which managed to coax a total of 470 horsepower from the engine.

BMW's famous Art Car treatments embellished the purposeful bodywork with imaginative designs from

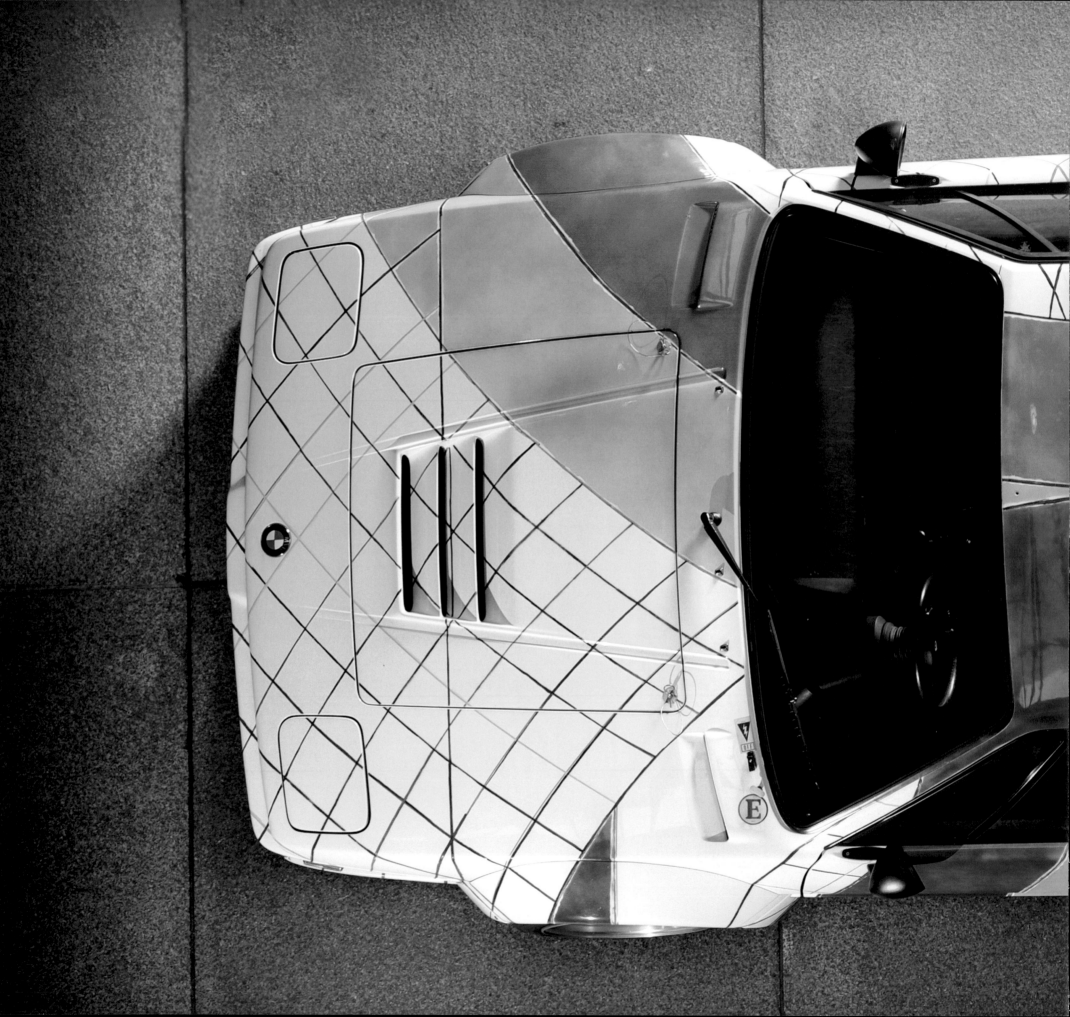

world-class artists including Roy Lichtenstein, Andy Warhol, and David Hockney. This particular example was ordered new by seven-time World Champion IMSA racer Peter Gregg. Artist Frank Stella was responsible for transforming the BMW's flat bodywork panels into rolling art with his so-called Polar Coordinates scheme, accentuating the M1's aesthetics with a signature look that would become among the most coveted of BMW's Art Car series, later taking pride of place for many years in the Solomon R. Guggenheim Museum collection in New York.

"*Sport and art have one key thing in common: in the end it comes down to satisfaction. My philosophy is always: give your best. Sometimes I'm surprised at what turns out, at other times I'm disappointed. Out here on the race track it's very hard not to be thrilled.*"

– Frank Stella

BMW M1
PRO-CAR

Engine:	3453 cc, 6-cylinder	**Chassis no.:**	9430-1053
Horsepower:	470		

Coachwork by Baur. Frank Stella "Polar Coordinates" Art Car for Peter Gregg. 1 of 16 Art Cars and the only private BMW–approved example. From the Guggenheim Museum Collection.

Sold at Bonhams Quail Lodge Auction, Carmel, August 2011, for $854,000.

1982
FERRARI *512 BBi*

"One of the most capable and exciting supercars of its era and capable of providing all the thrills that an enthusiastic owner–driver could wish for."

– *Classic Driver*

Based on Ferrari's 3-liter Formula 1 car, the 365 GT4 evolved into the 512 Berlinetta Boxer in 1976, which boasted a 5-liter flat-12. Featuring coachwork by Scaglietti and design by Pininfarina, the 512 BB incorporated Ferrari's first ever 180°, flat 12-cylinder engine in a production car, as well as the first belt-driven camshaft design from the manufacturer. As such, the engine produced 360 hp at 6200 rpm, fed by four 3-barrel Weber carburetors that were replaced by iniezione—or injection—in 1981, giving rise to the BBi.

Though Enzo Ferrari long resisted building mid-engined cars with 12-cylinder engines, Lamborghini's brawny Miura and Countach models inspired the famously headstrong leader to finally position a 12-cylinder power-plant amidships. The result was the 365 GT4 Berlinetta Boxer, which replaced the front-engine Daytona model with a 4.4-liter flat-12, producing 380 hp.

Unlike its more simplistic looking predecessor, the 512 BBi's taillight count dropped from six to four, while the bodywork added a chin spoiler and low drag air inlets. The resulting package not only looked the part, with a meaner stance and more aggressive bodywork, it was capable

of accelerating to 60 mph in 6 seconds flat and achieving a top speed of 188 mph, according to Ferrari. Standard items included a leather interior, electric windows, three-point inertia seatbelts, and air conditioning. Though it produced 40 fewer horsepower due to tightening US emissions regulations, the 512 BBi paved the way for a series of desirable mid-engined, 12-cylinder Ferraris including the Testarossa, which was produced from 1984 to 1991.

FERRARI 512 BBI

Engine:	4943 cc, 12-cylinder	**Chassis no.:**	ZFFJA09B000040999
Horsepower:	340	**Engine no.:**	110A00118

Coachwork by Scaglietti.

Sold at Bonhams Scottsdale Auction, Scottsdale, January 2015, for $357,500.

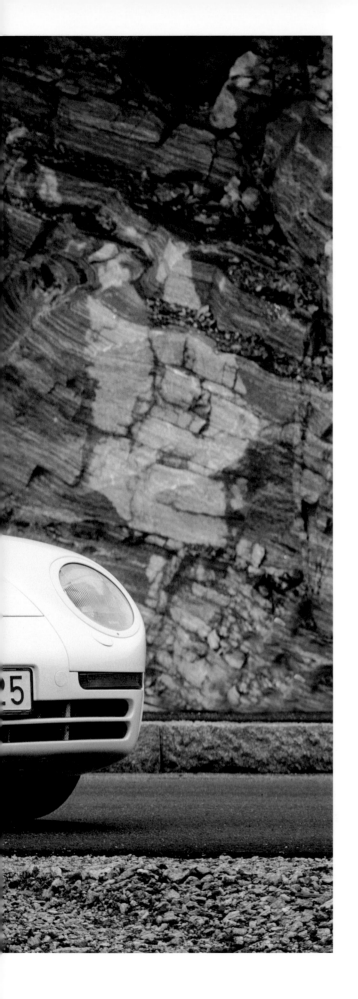

PORSCHE *959*

KOMFORT COUPE

The 959 quickly became notorious not only for its outstanding technological innovations but for its claim as the fastest production car on the planet.

2.85-liter, flat six-cylinder, liquid-cooled engine originally developed for the "Moby Dick" race car was a sophisticated all-wheel drive system that

The Porsche 959 debuted as a concept at the 1983 Frankfurt Motor Show and was intended to serve as a Gruppe B race car, though it went into production in 1986 purely as a street car available in two trims—Sport and Komfort. Though it was based on the 911 and visually resembled a more elaborately styled, authoritative version of that venerable platform, the 959's true benefits included sophisticated mechanical underpinnings and aluminum and Kevlar composite body panels for weight savings (including lightweight floor materials that replaced the 911's steel units) that helped trim overall mass to just over 3000 lbs (1361 kg). Assisting the 959's race-derived

helped lay power down by transferring up to 80 percent of power bias to the rear wheels.

The 959 quickly became notorious not only for its outstanding technological innovations but for its claim as the fastest production car on the planet (with the Sport model achieving a top speed of 197 mph). In addition to its advanced all-wheel drive system and signature engine, there was a new sequential turbocharger system that helped deliver power more aggressively (with a total of 444 lbs), creating a departure from Porsche's notoriously abrupt power delivery that earned previous vehicles a reputation for being snappy and difficult to wrangle. The result was

A dazzlingly ambitious vehicle that primed the world stage for a new wave of supercars.

a potent, groundbreaking package that set new limits for what enthusiasts could expect from production supercars and triggered a technological renaissance among auto-makers wishing to compete.

Though the 959 competed in and won the Dakar Rally in 1986—shocking the automotive industry—it will best be remembered as a dazzlingly ambitious vehicle that primed the world stage for a new wave of supercars.

PORSCHE 959
KOMFORT COUPE

Engine: 2849 cc, 6-cylinder **Chassis no.:** WPOZZZ95ZJ5900210
Horsepower: 450

Sold at Bonhams Bond Street Sale, London, December 2014,
for £505,500.

1993
FERRARI *F40 LM*
TWIN-TURBOCHARGED

"The fastest Ferrari of its day, and that alone guarantees its place among the greats… Its the ultimate must-have machine of its era—for so many reasons."

– *Classic & Performance Car*

Ferrari's F40 was a radical departure from the brand's typical road-going offerings, boasting competition-inspired construction that made the heavily ducted, scooped, and winged flagship more akin to a race car with license plates than a modified road car. As though the 478 horsepower F40 was not raucous enough, Ferrari concluded production by building a limited run of 19 competition-ready F40 LM models, which were named after the Le Mans circuit.

The F40 LM took the already brutal F40 to even more dizzying heights. While a factory tuning kit enabled an additional 200 horsepower to be extracted from the twin-turbocharged V8, the F40 LM boasted a staggering output of 700 bhp at 8100 rpm. The already stout chassis was reinforced, while more aggressive bodywork enabled greater downforce and enhanced engine cooling. Suspension was also tuned stiffer, brakes were uprated, and a race-ready gearbox transferred power to the F40 LM's larger wheels.

Despite its considerable weight savings through the use of high-tech carbon fiber, the F40 LM is still very much an analog supercar, boasting a lack of traction control and anti-lock brakes. The onus to extract the F40 LM's extraordinary performance falls upon the driver, with a conventional three-pedal manual gearbox, an unassisted steering system, and an ultra responsive accelerator pedal within reach.

Arguably the only thing more alluring than its raw speed is the Ferrari F40 LM's extreme rarity: offered to only 19 of the brand's most loyal customers, the F40 LM is scarcer than its legendary predecessor, the 250 GTO.

FERRARI F40 LM
TWIN-TURBOCHARGED

| **Engine:** | 2936 cc, 8-cylinder | **Chassis no.:** | ZFFGX34X000097893 |
| **Horsepower:** | 700 | **Engine no.:** | 17318-C |

Coachwork by Pininfarina. Number 18 of 19 total produced.

Sold at Bonhams Quail Lodge Auction, Carmel, August 2014, for $2,200,000.

1997
MCLAREN *F1 GTR*

"LONGTAIL"

> *"The fastest, most accelerative production car the world has ever seen."*
>
> – *Car and Driver*

The McLaren F1 went into production in 1992, looking and sounding like nothing else on the road or the track. Boasting an unconventional three-seater configuration, a staggering array of no compromises engineering, and an obsessively tailored vision for extreme performance and outright speed, the McLaren F1 made no apologies for its audacious road presence and take-no-prisoners performance.

Designed by South African Gordon Murray, the F1 was created with exotic materials and advanced construction, incorporating such novel features as a centrally positioned seat for the driver and twin Kevlar fans to create downforce. Featuring the world's first carbon fiber reinforced plastic monocoque, the F1 spared no expense to achieve its goals for road supremacy. Furthering the cost-is-no-object philosophy, gold insulating foil was installed around the engine bay to ensure optimal heat containment—all

of which helped the street car achieve a world record top speed of 240 mph (386 kph). Only 106 street legal F1s were built, paving the way for a remarkable but relatively short career in racing.

Powered by a naturally aspirated BMW 5900 cc V12, the F1's brutal power and sub-2500 pound (1134 kg) curb weight made it a fearsome machine that actually required de-tuning in order to be eligible to race at Le Mans, which it won in 1995. Following the success of the GTR race car, the F1 was once again converted for competition in 1997 into the more sophisticated GTR "Longtail" configuration, which lengthened the nose and tail sections while adding a wider rear wing for enhanced downforce. Aiding the car's proportions were wider wheel wells to accommodate larger tires for more lateral g-force holding. The engine's stroke

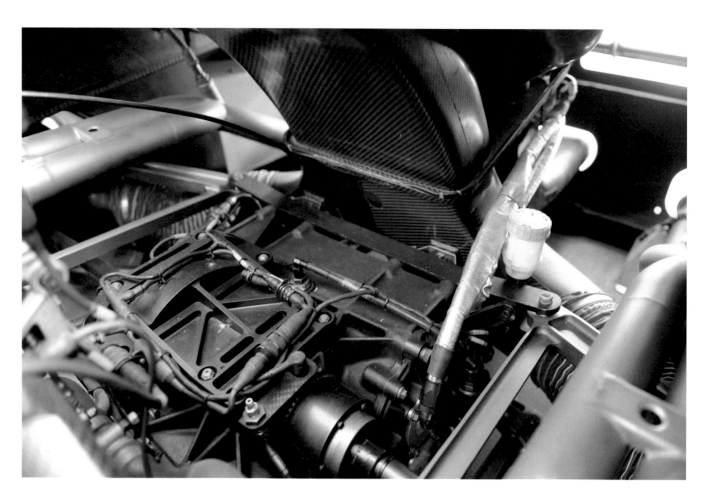

was also dropped, reducing displacement to 5990 cc in the interest of enhancing life during endurance races. Also aiding the race efforts was an Xtrac six-speed gearbox that may have lacked the manual's appealingly visceral driver experience but signaled the car's more focused performance. A total of only 28 GTR chassis were built.

This particular example, chassis number 028R, is clad in iconic Gulf livery and was run by the McLaren F1 GTR race program in eight premier-league FIA GT World Championship qualifying races, and achieved two points-scoring sixth place finishes. Following its racing career, the car returned to McLaren's headquarters in England and was preserved for several years before it was sold to Jim Gainer Racing in Japan in 2004. Equipped with the Xtrac gearbox, carbon Brembo brakes, and McLaren's unmistakable longtail bodywork, the F1 GTR represents the ultimate performance variant of the legendary model, and the final F1 ever built.

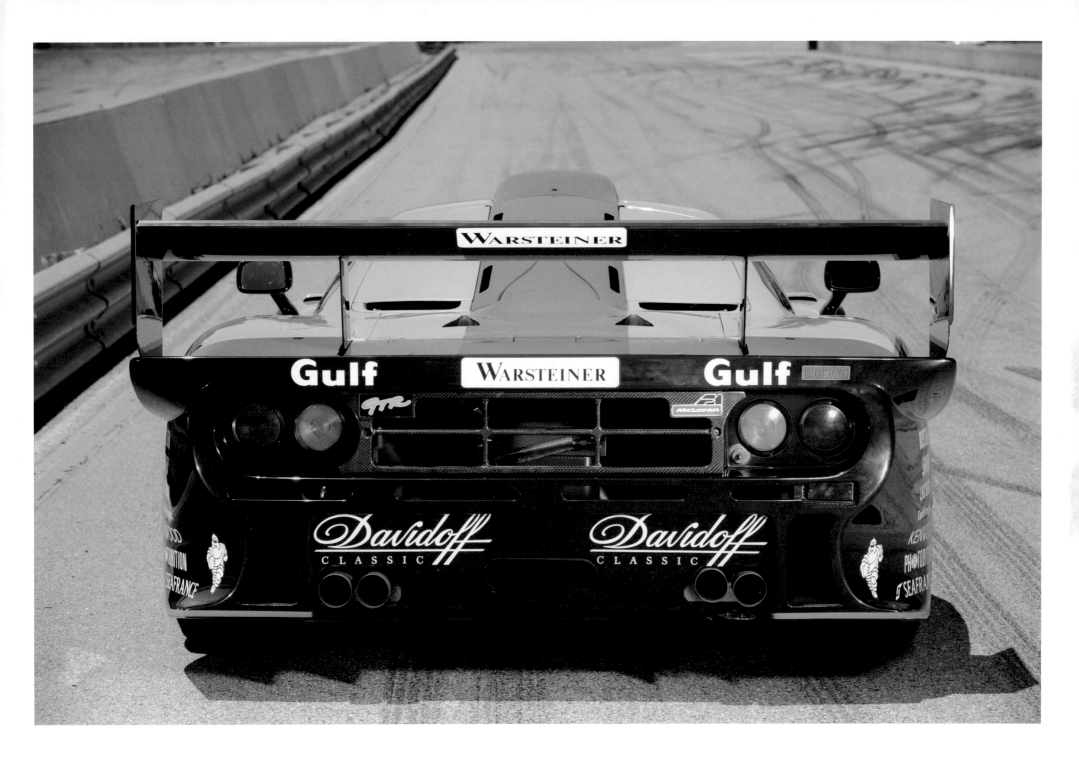

MCLAREN F1 GTR
"LONGTAIL"

Tenth and final example of the FIA GT race car.

Engine:	6.1-liter 12-cylinder	**Chassis no.:**	028R	Sold by Bonhams as a private treaty sale in 2012.
Horsepower:	550			

INDEX

THE BONHAMS
GUIDE TO CLASSIC
SPORTS & RACE CARS

Motoring Photographer Pawel Litwinski
After nearly a decade of specialization in this field, Pawel's work is easily recognized. His photographs show a unique brilliance (clarity) and depth. His artistry and instinct in his choice of location and angles evoke the period and particular qualities of each car that he shoots.
litwinski.com

GENTLEMEN, START YOUR ENGINES!
THE BONHAMS GUIDE TO CLASSIC SPORTS & RACE CARS

This book was conceived, edited, and designed by Gestalten.

Edited by Jared Zaugg and Robert Klanten
All texts by Jared Zaugg
Additional profile texts by Basem Wasef (pp. 268–281, 288–317)
Preface by Jared Zaugg and James Knight

Editorial management by Vanessa Obrecht
Layout and design by Sarah Peth
Cover by Vanessa Obrecht
Cover photography by Pawel Litwinski
Typefaces: Adobe Caslon Pro by Carol Twombly, Engel by Gestalten Fonts,
Calibri by Lucas de Groot
Proofreading by Felix Lennert

© all images: Bonhams and the photographers

Printed by Optimal Media GmbH, Röbel / Müritz
Made in Germany

Published by Gestalten, Berlin 2015
ISBN: 978-3-89955-567-7

2nd printing, 2016

Respect copyrights, encourage creativity!

For more information, please visit www.gestalten.com.

Bibliographic information published by the Deutsche Nationalbibliothek.
The Deutsche Nationalbibliothek lists this publication in the Deutsche
Nationalbibliografie;
detailed bibliographic data are available online at http://dnb.d-nb.de.

None of the content in this book was published in exchange for payment by
commercial parties or designers; Gestalten selected all included work based
solely on its artistic merit.

This book was printed on paper certified by the FSC®.

FSC
www.fsc.org

MIX
Paper from
responsible sources
FSC® C108521